20 Ways To
Enjoy Life More
As A Christian

Biblical and Practical Changes to

Significantly Improve Your Life

DEMETRA MUINGBEH

DEDICATION

I would like to dedicate this book to the two people who have supported me without fail over the years – my amazing parents, Kenneth and Regina Minor. Thank you both for your love, your example of faith, and your constant prayers.

Dad, your love and passion for learning, teaching, and preaching the Word of God has been a daily inspiration to me. What God has done and is doing in your life remains one of the most influential testimonies that encourages me along my own Christian journey.

Mom, you are one of the strongest women I know. Your strength, virtue, humility, kindness, and patience continue to be an awesome example for me. Knowing what you've endured, and how God uses you to be such a blessing in the lives of others, motivates me to surrender more and more of myself to Him to be used for His purpose.

I love you both more than words can express.

CONTENTS

INTRODUCTION

Ever had a bad day? A bad week? A bad month? Or maybe you can't even remember the last time things weren't bad in your life. This is so often the case among many Christians. We give our lives to Christ and accept him as our Lord and Savior, only to simply exist on earth as if we never had.

We let things like waking up late, a disobedient child, traffic on the way to work, spilled coffee, a lost ATM card, a flat tire, a co-worker's nasty attitude, or a rude text message dictate how we feel for an entire day! Thankfully, all those things typically don't happen all in the same day. However, we know how just one event can set us off. Then that one event turns into us professing another "bad day". Although, none of these things are fun to experience, they don't have to ruin our lives. The issue with these "bad days" is that they tend to pile up and snowball our lives. We constantly give up on today and just wait for tomorrow.

God did not intend for us as Christians to go through life held hostage by our circumstances. Regardless of what is going on in our lives, we have been given everything we need to be successful in our walk with Him and to enjoy life to the fullest in the process. Peace, joy, strength, patience, endurance (just to name a few) are ours in Christ!

Yes, there are going to be tough times for everyone. Sometimes it will be minor, like getting a paper cut, having a bad interview, or losing your favorite earrings. Other times it will be major, like getting bad results from a medical test, losing a job, or having your spouse decide they want a divorce. Whatever challenges may come, you don't have to let them dictate your outlook on life. There are things you can do to start making your days better and to start enjoying your life more.

The problem is, we accept and settle for mediocre lives. I'm not talking about material possessions. After all, some of the most miserable people on the planet are those that have tons of money, homes, cars, etc. I'm talking about Christians settling for living lives far short of what God intended for us to have. Living with constant defeat, fear, worry, stress, anger, bitterness, negativity, and lack of discipline that leads us to be miserable far too often.

It's so frustrating living like that – trust me, I've been there! Realizing that God can help me have better days despite what is going on around me, was one of the most liberating revelations in my Christian life. I had spent so many years depressed, discouraged, angry and disappointed that I wasn't where I wanted to be in life. It wasn't until God showed me in His Word that life isn't really about what *we* want out of life, but rather about what *He* wants for us. The funny part is, what He wants for us, is far better than anything we could plan for ourselves! It's when we start listening to Him, and allowing Him to direct our lives, that we start to barely even notice the circumstances around us and start to enjoy our lives to the fullest, the way He intended us to.

John 10:10 (AMP) says, "I came that they may have and enjoy life, and have it in abundance [to the full, till it overflows]." God never intended for us to simply exist on earth. In fact, this verse tells us that Jesus came so that we may have true life and enjoy it to the fullest! There is no way this entails the misery that so many of us have allowed to become a part of our daily lives.

My goal with this book is to help you learn how to enjoy the life that Jesus died for us to have, and to encourage you in the process. There are 20 biblical and practical changes that you can start making in your life to start seeing significant improvements. Instead of letting bad days continue to waste and ruin your life, let's start taking proactive measures and utilize the tools God has already given us to begin to enjoy life the way He intended. As for those of you who think you are already enjoying life, I promise you, that you ain't seen nothing yet!

Although this can be a quick read, I encourage you to take your time. Read each chapter thoroughly. Meditate on the verses used. Complete and apply the tasks listed in the "Putting it into Practice" sections. And expect the unexpected as God begins to work in your life – because I assure you, He is about to do something new and great!

SECTION I:

Cultivate Your Faith

His divine power has given us everything we need for a godly life through our knowledge of him who called us by his own glory and goodness.

II Peter 1:3

Everything we need to be *truly* successful and enjoy this thing called the "Christian Life" stems from the Word of God. Without it we are simply co-existing with non-believers on earth until we get to heaven.

CHAPTER 1

Embrace the Bible

Your word is a lamp for my feet, a light on my path.

Psalm 119:105

DID YOU KNOW……

The Bible:

- is the very Word of God
- is a collection of 66 books (39 in the Old Testament, 27 in the New Testament)
- was written over a period of 1600 years (from about 1500 BC to AD 100)
- was written by approximately 40 different authors (kings, prophets, leaders, followers of God)
- has 31,101 verses
- has 783,137 to 788,280 words (depending on what version you're reading)
- was first put into print in 1455 with Johannes Gutenberg's printing press
- has approximately 1,260 promises
- has approximately 6,468 commands
- has been translated into more than 3,000 languages
- is sold, given away or distributed in the U.S. 168,000 times daily!

How has such a book become so irrelevant, undervalued, and underutilized among Christians today?

I just can't seem to wrap my head around the fact that we live in a world today where the Bible is depicted as such. The very thing we disregard most, is the very thing that could change our lives so drastically for the better. It is not just a book of instructions or rules. It truly is *the* guidebook for our lives. Show me a "miserable Christian" and I guarantee he or she is also a non-bible reading Christian. On the other hand, show me a Christian who is truly enjoying life the way God intended us to, and I guarantee he or she embraces the Word of God regularly in their lives.

Having been a Christian myself for 28 years, I can honestly say, that it wasn't until this last decade that I began to really embrace the bible for what it really was. And, I can absolutely, without a shadow of a doubt, promise any fellow Christian, that if you begin to embrace the Word of God regularly, then you will begin to enjoy your life more than ever before! I'm more than a witness!

But, that sounds so...... basic, simple, almost even hard to really believe. You mean to tell me that if I start reading this ancient book regularly that my problems are going to vanish, blessings are going to rain down on me, and I will never experience pain again?

Pause. STOP! No! None of *that* is what I'm saying at all. I'm saying, that if you want to cultivate a better relationship with God and enjoy life the way He intended you to enjoy it, that it all starts with allowing Him to speak to you through His Word – regularly.

Sadly, Christians often allow our society to dictate how much of God we need in our lives.

Christians always seem to overlook and even challenge this truth. In fact, many readers of this book will ignore this chapter altogether and jump right to implementing some of the other things instead. We don't realize, that all the other things actually stem from this one basic step. Yes, you can implement everything else that I will mention throughout this book, and you'll even start to see good results. However, I promise, you will be even more successful, in a shorter period of time, if you start here.

Jesus himself, told his disciples in Matthew 4:4, "Man shall not live on bread alone, but on every word that comes from the mouth of God."

How can we live according to the Word if we have no clue what it says? Truly enjoying life on a consistent basis, as a Christian, MUST include a change in our attitude about the bible. We cannot neglect God's Word and expect Him to bless us with everything we want out of life. I promise that the moment you begin to embrace His Word for what it truly is, not only will God begin to change your perspective on life, but He will begin to bless you in ways you weren't even thinking about before.

And by the way, I only guarantee these things because the bible guarantees them. Scripture is very clear about the many benefits of incorporating God's Word into our lives.

10 Key Benefits of Reading the Bible:

- It shows us how to obey and live for God (John 14:15; II Timothy 3:16-17)
- Spiritual nourishment and growth (I Peter 2:2-3; John 6:35)
- Wisdom and guidance for life (Psalm 119:105)
- Peace and comfort (Psalm 119:50, 165; Isaiah 26:3)
- Hope and healing (Psalm 107:19-20; 119:47, 114; 130:5)
- Endurance and strength during difficult times (Psalm 119:28, 92, 143)
- Blessings and success (Joshua 1:7; Psalm 119:2; Luke 11:28)
- Discernment of truth (John 8:31-32; Acts 20:29-31; I Timothy 4:1; John 4:1)
- It keeps us from sin (Psalm 119:9, 11)
- It helps us fight spiritual battles (Ephesians 6:10-17; II Corinthians 10:3-4)

Are any of the things listed above important to you? Are any of them missing from your life?

At the lowest and darkest point in my entire life (and yes, I was a Christian at the time), when I had lost seemingly everything, and even contemplated thoughts of suicide, it was the Word of God that truly saved my life.

I had no one to turn to that I could really express the depth of the pain and hurt I was feeling at the time. I didn't know what to do and I honestly felt like I was going to lose my mind. One day with the tiniest ounce of strength I had, and with tears in my eyes, I picked up my bible. I didn't know where to start or even have the energy to read. So I just opened up to page one in Genesis.

For days I laid in bed. Lights off. Crying. But somehow, I managed to saturate myself with God's Word in the midst of it – only a few minutes at a time. My problems did not dissolve overnight. The pain, sorrow, anguish, fear, doubt, shame, and stress certainly didn't vanish either. But God, through His Word, and the presence of His Spirit within me, held me tightly every single one of those dark days. Giving me a little glimpse of light that shined a little brighter each day.

The full story is perhaps another book, for another time. But here I stand, 8 years later, stronger than ever and truly enjoying life! I don't regret the experience at all. *That* is the power of God's Word. And NOTHING else on earth compares to it.

Now, that's just a piece of my testimony. But, what can the Word of God do in *your* life if you just allow it to? What if you could significantly improve and enjoy your life more, simply by spending more time reading the bible? What do you have to lose? When are you going to get started?

Putting it into Practice

Where do I start reading? I'm glad you asked!

- ➤ Although, Psalms 119 is the longest chapter in the Bible, its a great place to start, since it talks about the importance of the Word of God and the benefits of it.
- ➤ Take some time and look up all the verses mentioned in this chapter. Meditate on them.

> ➤ I also challenge you to take the verses mentioned throughout this book and use them as a starting place to commit verses to memory.
> ➤ For reading the bible in general, I would suggest starting with the book of Psalms, Proverbs or John.
> ➤ For those of you who prefer to do everything online or via your phone - there are also hundreds of devotional and bible apps that exist. Google is your friend.
> ➤ If you simply get started, God will do the rest. Give it 30 days and see how God will begin to do things in your life, and how you will begin to enjoy it more – guaranteed!

WARNING

Simply reading the bible, could easily turn into a strong desire to read more and more. Possible side effects include, but are not limited to: daily devotions, meditating, verse memorization, wanting to go to bible study and even church, people looking at you like you're weird, and you thinking that you're weird. Please consult a pastor or elder if you start to literally *embrace* your bible.

DO NOT stop using this product once it begins to give the desired effects. Withdrawal may result in increased stress, worry, frustration, misery, depression, fear, pain, doubt, and spiritual fatigue. These symptoms will not diminish unless re-treated immediately with this product.

CHAPTER 2

Converse With God

*Rejoice always, pray continually, give thanks in all circumstances;
for this is God's will for you in Christ Jesus.*

I Thessalonians 5:16-18

Whew! Another day. Thank you! I'm sooooooo tired. Definitely could have used an extra hour of sleep, and definitely not looking forward to doing these massive reports at work today. But together, I know we got this. I know my attitude has sucked lately. Please forgive me, and help me to be in a better mood today. It's just that Veronica is always acting like such a you know what, but I know I need to stop letting her get to me. I get angry, then I get frustrated, then I go home mad and take it out on the kid. Ughhhh…..but today is free slurpee day at 7-Eleven. Woohoo, I can go at lunch time. Thank you for the small things (laughter). Ok God, this is it, another Wednesday, 8 hours to put in. Please just give me strength. I know you got me.

That was my exact conversation with God one morning as I sat in the parking lot outside of where I worked. I had arrived 15 minutes early that day and didn't want to go in until I absolutely had to. So as usual, I used some of my free minutes to talk to God. I didn't have to formulate any special spiritual words. I didn't even bow my head or close my eyes. That's the best part about a relationship with God – He's always there – watching and listening.

Christians tend to complicate what prayer really is. Simply put, prayer is talking to God. Having a conversation with Him. It's not a speech, or formal monologue that we have to write out first to perfect or practice. He is our Heavenly Father and we are His children. He has given us total and complete access to Him 24/7. Next to His Word, prayer is the other most powerful tool that goes neglected amongst Christians.

Most of us use it when we need something, want something, or have gotten ourselves into some trouble and have nowhere else to turn. Very few utilize our relationship with Him to reap the benefits that would help us enjoy life more.

Imagine having access and authority to call on the creator of all things, at any given moment. Imagine Him listening attentively, as you talk to Him about any and everything going on in your life. Your hurts, your fears, your secrets, your struggles, your weaknesses. The ability to laugh, cry, or even scream if necessary, never having to pretend that you're ok when you're not. Now, stop imagining, because as Christians it is our reality!

Scripture not only tells us to pray, but it says we should pray *continually*. In fact, it is actually God's will that we do so.

In chapter 1 we learned that God wants to speak to us through His Word. And guess what? He wants us to talk to Him just as much. Our relationship with God isn't just us believing He died for our sins, accepting Him as our Lord and Savior, and saying 'thanks, I'll see you in heaven'. It's a relationship that needs to be cultivated just like any other relationship we have, especially if we want it to grow.

I used to struggle with praying. There was no time, or I couldn't find the right quiet spot, or I didn't know what to say. It wasn't until I simply just started talking to God, that a few words became conversations. Conversations that I could have with Him, whether I was at home, in class, at work, at the gym, in the grocery store, standing in line at the bank, in the McDonalds drive thru, or while I was washing dishes. I would just talk to him about any and everything that came to mind – my day (the good and bad), how I was feeling, what I needed, what I was grateful for, prayers for others, etc.

We all know how awkward it is when you try to force a relationship with someone. You never know what to say around the person. There is no reason for us to have that issue in our relationship with God. After all, He created us. He knows everything about us, including our flaws. He simply wants us to be our authentic selves and invite Him into our daily lives. He wants us to converse with Him – and He will listen – always.

James 4:8 (NLT) says, "Come close to God, and God will come close to you." What better way is there to get closer to God than by spending more time reading His Word and conversing with Him regularly. The problem is that we want God, and even expect God, to just work in our lives.

We want all the blessings and privileges that come with our spiritual relationship, but we want it without having to spend time with Him.

The good news, is that by default, there are certain blessings that simply come with being a child of God. However, there are so many other blessings available to us that would allow us to enjoy life even more if we simply seek to grow in our relationship with God. I mean really, how hard is it to make time for the one who gives us life? And what are we missing out on because we refuse to give Him that time?

Conversing with God is NEVER wasted time. I guarantee if you start talking to Him more, even if it's just a few minutes each day, you will start to see a major difference in your relationship with Him and in your life. If talking to God more will help you to enjoy life more, why wouldn't you make it a priority to do so?

<u>Putting it into Practice</u>

- If you don't know how to begin, start with 'Hey God, it's me (<u>your name</u>)', and go from there!
- Read Jesus' example of prayer in Matthew 6:9-13.
- Tell Him what you're thankful for (name any and everything that comes to mind).
- Talk to Him about what's on your mind (struggles, problems, fears, questions, etc.).
- Talk to Him about what you need and want (personally, financially, physically, goals/dreams)

> ➢ Ask Him to direct you as to what He wants you to do in general
> ➢ Pray for your spiritual growth. Ask Him to give you a hunger and desire for His Word.

WARNING

Conversing with God can lead to a desire for longer conversations, talking out loud even when you're in a public place, and the desire to take "prayer breaks" at work.

Possible side effects include, but are not limited to: people thinking you are losing your mind, answered prayers, additional blessings, sudden moments of crying, laughter, or outbursts.

CHAPTER 3

Trust and Obey

Trust in and rely confidently on the Lord with all your heart and do not rely on your own insight or understanding. In all your ways know and acknowledge and recognize Him, and He will make your paths straight and smooth [removing obstacles that block your way].

Proverbs 3:5-6 (AMP)

Once you're at the point where you're beginning to read the bible and converse with God, you will most definitely begin to hear from God more often. Whether it's through the verses you're reading, or Him confirming something He has already told you from His Word though another person, God will start directing you in different areas of your life.

The verses above tell us that we are to trust in God with all our heart, and acknowledge Him in all our ways. Trust is not an easy thing to establish with anyone, including God. We know as Christians that we should trust Him. However, we don't automatically wake up just trusting God for everything.

When I lost my husband, home, job, car, and ministry all within a one year time-span, I can tell you that I didn't wake up with a giant smile on my face saying 'it's all good, I'm trusting in the Lord, and He's got me'. Although, He definitely had me, I certainly didn't feel like it at the time. I was lost, ashamed, depressed, stressed, angry, bitter, scared, confused, and even questioning if God was still there. So often our advice to people when they are going through things is 'oh, you just have to trust in God'. Well, I'm here to tell you that its easier said than done.

The good news is, the more we cultivate our relationship with God, the more we can *build* our trust in Him. I am grateful to say that I didn't stay in that depressed, miserable state too long when my life got turned upside down. That was only because I began to embrace God and His

Word more than I had ever done before – and that was what turned things around for me. At my lowest point in life, God reminded me through His Word, that He was still there, that He would never leave me, and that I could trust Him to help me get back on track again.

So often we put our trust in others, in material possessions, and even in ourselves. But ultimately all those things will fail us at some point. There are going to be so many days in this life where we simply will have no other option, or anyone to turn to but God. It will be in those moments where the willingness to trust in Him will become most important.

There are so many promises in the bible – promises that God will protect us, provide for us, deliver us from trouble, watch over our households, bless us, etc. When we know God's Word to be true and His promises to be real, we will learn to trust Him more and more. And when we start trusting Him, that will lead to obedience. Trusting His Word and doing what it says goes hand in hand.

In fact, I Samuel 15:22 tells us, to obey is better than sacrifice. God desires our obedience to His Word more than our "good deeds".

It is when we start to put all these concepts together – embracing the bible, conversing with God, trusting, and obeying His Word – that we truly begin to cultivate our faith. When we cultivate our faith, then watch out, because that is when our lives truly begin to change, improve, and get better. We may *think* we have been happy, life has been good, and we're in a good place. But, God wants to take our simple happiness to a level of joy.

Happiness is determined by what is going on around you. Joy, however, is something you can have even on your worst day.

God doesn't want our lives to just be good, but great – amazing even! John 10:10 (a verse I will reiterate several times throughout this book), says "I came that they may have and enjoy life, and have it in abundance [to the full, till it overflows]."

I don't know about you, but if I can change, enhance and improve my life, simply by cultivating my faith and relationship with God, I don't have to think twice about doing it. Such simple things, yet so easy to neglect, overlook and put aside.

People look for shortcuts to blessings all day, every day. Well, I'm giving you some practical shortcuts right here to enjoying life more – starting NOW. The question is, will you utilize them?

Putting it into Practice

➢ Find 10 verses where the word "trust" is listed in the bible. Read and meditate on those verses.

➢ Make a list of the top 3 areas where you struggle to trust God (i.e. finances, health, education, etc.). Turn the list into a daily prayer list and ask God to help you begin to trust Him in those areas of your life.

➢ Are there any major life decisions that you are in the midst of making right now? Have you acknowledged God about it yet? Spend some time talking to God about it, so He can direct you accordingly.

➢ Is there anything you have read lately in the bible that God has asked you to do, but you haven't done it yet? Talk to Him about it, ask for His strength to help you do it, and go get it done.

➢ Have you been in a rut, and feel like you're alone, and that you can't even talk to God, let alone trust Him about anything right now? Go back and re-read chapter 1. Then start reading the book of Psalms.

WARNING

Trusting and obeying God can lead to a significant increase in your level of faith. Possible side effects include, but are not limited to: believing anything in life is possible, making decisions that don't quite make sense to others, taking risks that God tells you to, ridicule from others who don't believe in God, family and friends thinking you're nuts, increased blessings and levels of joy. Please continue use of this product even if you feel like you are "over-trusting" or reaping too many benefits. It will NOT kill you.

SECTION II:

Acknowledge Life's Challenges

*And we know that in all things God works
for the good of those who love him,
who have been called according to his purpose.*

Romans 8:28

When it comes to facing difficult situations, God has taught me to acknowledge some of life's challenges that every Christian will encounter. If we acknowledge them, we won't be too caught off guard when things happen. God will equip us with what we need to overcome every obstacle, while we continue to enjoy life in the process.

CHAPTER 4

Beware of the Devil

*Be alert and of sober mind. Your enemy the devil prowls around
like a roaring lion looking for someone to devour.*

I Peter 5:8

The bible teaches that our enemy the devil is not only real, but that he ultimately wants to devour us as Christians. The word *devour* means to eat prey hungrily or to destroy completely. Whatever way you look at it, the devil is NOT our friend. In fact, His sole purpose is to destroy our walk with God!

I Peter 5:8 uses the imagery of a roaring lion on the prowl to describe the devil. A lion is known to be a very patient animal, as they will literally lay in wait for hours for their prey. They are also known for their stealth like attacks as they tend to maintain the element of surprise (despite their size) before they prance on their prey, and devour them completely. This is exactly how the devil works in our lives as Christians.

He is very patient and subtle, only to come out of nowhere and attack us in ways we least expect. In his patience, he learns and studies our weaknesses and our "pressure points", so that he can use them against us. He will play on our emotions, influence people around us, and manipulate situations and circumstances just to get us to be susceptible to his attacks.

In order to enjoy life more, we must acknowledge the existence of the devil, and his work in the world we live in. If we don't, then we will automatically set ourselves up for failure and a life of misery. Ephesians 6:11-17 says:

"Put on the full armor of God, so that you can take your stand against the devil's schemes. For our struggle is not against flesh and blood, but against the rulers, against the authorities, against the powers of this dark world and against the spiritual forces of evil in the heavenly realms. Therefore put on the full armor of God, so that when the day of evil comes, you may be able to stand your ground, and after you have done everything, to stand. Stand firm then, with the belt of truth buckled around your waist, with the breastplate of righteousness in place, and with your feet fitted with the readiness that comes from the gospel of peace. In addition to all this, take up the shield of faith, with which you can extinguish all the flaming arrows of the evil one. Take the helmet of salvation and the sword of the Spirit, which is the word of God."

This passage teaches us about the spiritual war that is going on behind the scenes of our lives and how to fight accordingly. We can't fight a *spiritual* war with *physical* weapons. So often, we as Christians try to solve all the wrongs going on in our lives, and in the world around us by human means. However, we have been given spiritual weapons that God has told us to learn to fight with instead.

Whether it's a domestic abuse situation, a bitter angry uncle who has been holding a grudge for years, a business partner who continues to steal from you, political injustice, or racism, there are spiritual forces working behind the scenes. II Corinthians 10: 3-4 says:

"For though we live in the world, we do not wage war as the world does. The weapons we fight with are not the weapons of the world. On the contrary, they have divine power to demolish strongholds."

There are several points to emphasize here. As Christians:
- We don't have to let things affect us negatively the way non-believers do – reciprocating the same hate, racism, violence or evil.
- We have the capability to deal with issues on a spiritual level – exhibiting love, prayer, and speaking the Word.
- Our spiritual weapons actually work! They are guaranteed to demolish strongholds.

Of course, the key to all of this is that we have to actually start utilizing the weapons God has provided for us. It's so easy to get caught up in our emotions, and want to lash out in rage or violence when things happen around us. It is also so cliché to say 'just pray about it'. However, sometimes that is exactly all we need to do.

It's not that we are giving up, or being nonchalant, or not taking matters seriously. We go to God in prayer and read His Word to seek guidance on how to deal with our circumstances. When we turn these situations over to him, we acknowledge that the situation is bigger than us, and we open the door for God to change it. Again, putting everything together that we've learned in this book so far – the word, prayer, and trust – and now utilizing our tools to combat our enemy the devil, is the ONLY way to be successful and enjoy life in the process.

The bible tells us all about the devil's schemes and tactics. How exactly does he want to devour us? By stealing our joy, our peace, our patience, our sanity, our hope, our health, by tempting our kids to get into trouble, by using friends to bring up our past, by meddling with our finances, by causing things to go wrong in our lives in general – the list is endless.

For every person who decides to follow God as their Lord and Savior, the devil loses. He can't take that relationship from us, but he sure can try to ensure that our "Christian lives" our just as miserable as our lives would be without God. The further he can get us away from God's Word, the more he keeps us away from learning how to overcome him.

In order to enjoy life more, we must stay alert by keeping our spiritual eyes and ears in tune to what is going on around us.

We know the devil exists. We know his mission. We know how to fight him. We just have to start utilizing what God has given us, and then there will be no reason for us to fail and be miserable.

It is definitely a process. Just like a soldier trains before going into battle, if we cultivate our faith and our relationship with God, the stronger we will become over time to stand up against the devil. When you know your enemy, study his tactics, and then learn how to maximize your weapons, victory is always guaranteed! Let's start by making a decision today to stop letting the devil win and to start enjoying life more!

<u>*Putting it into Practice*</u>

- ➤ Read these verses that talk about the devil and his strategies:
  - John 8:44
  - II Corinthians 11:14
  - Matthew 4:1-11
  - II Corinthians 2:10-11
- ➤ Reflect on this previous week and identify ways in which the devil has been working in your life (situation at home/work, obstacle that came up that made you angry, a temptation that you gave in to). Then write down how you can better handle those situations going forward.
- ➤ Make a list of the areas of your life where you feel like the devil is winning right now (marriage, relationship with your kids, your health, your business, your job, etc.). Start committing those things to God in prayer and asking Him to guide you to work on them.
- ➤ Write down the following victory verses (on a post-it, index card, paper) and post them somewhere visible until you memorize them. Whenever you start to feel like you are losing, quote/read them:
  - Romans 8:31: "What, then, shall we say in response to these things? If God is for us, who can be against us?"
  - Romans 8:37: "No, in all these things we are more than conquerors through him who loved us."
  - I John 4:4: "You, dear children, are from God and have overcome them, because the one who is in you is greater than the one who is in the world."
  - Philippians 4:13: "I can do all this through him who gives me strength."
- ➤ Start keeping a journal of your moments of victory and praise God for them!

WARNING

Utilizing the armor of God and spiritual weapons will prove successful no matter how many times you use them. Sharpening them and reloading on a daily basis is recommended, although they can NEVER be over-used or worn out.

Possible side effects include, but are not limited to: increased appetite to learn more about your enemy and his tactics, increased ability to thwart his attacks, increased desire to pray instead of react to things emotionally, and more enjoyable days.

Please continue use of this product even if you feel like the devil has stopped bothering you for a while. He is simply trying to come up with new tactics. Stay alert and ready!

CHAPTER 5

Realize "Blah" Happens

The righteous person may have many troubles,
but the Lord delivers him from them all.

Psalm 34:19

If anyone has ever told you being a Christian was easy, or that it would eliminate all problems from your life, they lied. In fact, the bible tells us in numerous places that we will definitely face difficulties. Psalms 34:19 above tells us that we may have "many" troubles.

This is another one of life's challenges that we must acknowledge if we are going to truly enjoy life. If we approach life with the attitude that there is nothing that could, or should ever come up in our lives, we set ourselves up for failure.

Even our best laid plans and intentions can't keep bad stuff from happening. Some days are simply going to be better than others. There will be times when things just won't go our way. Unexpected situations will arise, people will disappoint you out of the blue, and more often than not, we'll disappoint ourselves.

I've had several "blah" days and even weeks. I've fallen off my diet, or didn't work out as much as I should have. I didn't do any blog posts. I didn't hit my supplemental income goal. I yelled at my kid several times for no reason. I sometimes slack off at work and then get behind. I don't complete half my errands because I simply don't feel like it. I literally just get in a negative, unmotivated, lazy rut, which leads to me getting little to nothing done. A week passes, and I'm frustrated, angry, upset, and disappointed.

Then there are those lovely moments where you feel like you are on cloud nine. Nothing but smiles and rainbows. You feel good, look good, and everything around you is just falling into place nicely. Until someone says something at work that makes you doubt your capabilities. Then you're in a bad mood for the remainder of the day. Which leads to road rage on your way home. You hit a pothole way too hard and get a flat tire. Then you call your spouse to pick you up, and you both argue the whole way home. Only to be greeted by the kids, who tell you the dog just died.

Your wallet is stolen. You didn't get approved for financial aid. Your son has been kicked off the football team. You're fired from your job. Your significant other breaks up with you out of the blue. There's an eviction notice taped to your door. Your teenage daughter is pregnant. A fire started at your house and burned half the place down. Your bank account is hacked and hundreds of dollars has been stolen. You find out you will never walk again after being injured in an accident. Your aunt is diagnosed with cancer. Your cousin never paid you back. Your addicted spouse gambled the rent money away again. A loved one passes away, and you never got to say goodbye.

The list of things that could happen to us in this life is infinite. And not one of these scenarios is pleasant, or fun to go through. So how are we supposed to enjoy life in the midst of such things? The enjoyment comes not *during* the experience of it all, but rather in knowing that God will carry us through it.

The bible says He *delivers* us from our troubles. It's not like Superman swooping down from the sky to immediately carry us away from the situation, and resolving things on the spot. God's deliverance always starts with His presence. Which is sometimes the ONLY thing that gives us just the strength we need to push through our circumstances.

You see Psalms 37:23-24 (NLT) says, "The Lord directs the steps of the godly. He delights in every detail of their lives. Though they stumble, they will never fall, for the Lord holds them by the hand." This verse is a reminder of the fact that not only am I going to have "blah" days or weeks, but that God is going to be with me through each and every one of them, holding my hand, and giving me the strength to get back on track again.

Life is hard. That's a fact. It's only because of our relationship with God that we can truly live with a purpose and enjoy life amidst the chaos that surrounds us.

Accept that you're not perfect, and will sometimes fall short. Accept that the people around you aren't perfect either, and that they will sometimes disappoint you. Accept that things will not always go the way you plan them to. And most of all, accept that even the "blah" days are a part of God's plan for you, and that with Him by your side you can face it all.

On the flip side of things, I have to also address my fellow Christians, that so often try to give the impression that they have it all together. That they're doing everything so flawlessly. That life is just awesome, every day and all the time. That they don't struggle, get discouraged, lonely, frustrated, worried, fed up, or even depressed sometimes. The truth remains that in our humanity, we all will have our highs and lows – whether its physical, emotional, mental, spiritual, relational, financial, or circumstantial.

I don't know about you, but I know and willingly admit, that I don't have it all together. I've got a lot to learn, a lot to overcome, and a lot of molding left for God to do in my life. But thankfully, I have a God who loves me, never leaves me, holds my hands through my not-so-good days, and forgives me for my sins. And according to the God's Word, that is what will get me through any "blah" day!

Express your emotions, be sad, cry it out, hit a punching bag if you need to, or find an open space and just scream. Let it all out. There is nothing wrong with that. Just don't stay in that mode forever.

The "blah" days will continue to come. Just cling to God, embrace His Word, and allow Him to carry you amidst the different situations. He's got way too much to do in our lives, for us to allow the circumstances of life to steal our joy. As a matter of fact, sometimes the "blah" is meant to teach us something, or serve as a stepping stone to something good God has in store for us!

With God, we will push through it all, move forward and continue to enjoy life!

Putting it into Practice

- ➢ Meditate on the verses below regarding not so pleasant circumstance or situations that may arise:
  - Deuteronomy 31:8 (God never leaves us)
  - Philippians 4:12-13 (unpleasant circumstances)
  - Hebrews 12:5-7 (God's discipline)
  - James 1:2-4 (trials/tribulations for Christ's sake)
  - II Corinthians 12:10 (when we are weak, He is strong)
- ➢ Reflect on your last "blah" moment, day, or week. How did you feel? How long did those feelings last? What could you have done to break out of that state of mind?
- ➢ Start to be cognizant of changes in your mood when things happen around you, that don't go your way or upsets you. Keep a journal for a few weeks. Write down what sets you off, how you react, and how long you stay in that mood.
- ➢ Ask God to help you have a better attitude and to begin to handle situations differently.
- ➢ Identify and make a list of any circumstances or situations in your life currently that seem to have you stuck in "blah" mode. (situation at work, at home, in school, with your finances, etc.). Start committing those things to God in prayer and asking for His help to resolve or move past the situation.
  NOTE: it could be something that has happened a long time ago that is still affecting you now.
- ➢ Also write down what God is teaching you through these situations. Give Him praise for your moments of victory and when He starts to renew your joy!

WARNING

Possible side effects of changing your attitude towards the "blah" of life include, but are not limited to: increased desire to smile or burst into laughter, a decrease in blood pressure, less stress lines, reduced number of headaches, a severe drop in anger, depression, and frustration.

NOTE: this product is highly CONTAGIOUS. Your abrupt change in attitude can severely impact and change the negativity around you!

Don't be surprised if continued use of this product gets you to the point where you barely even notice some of the "blah" that exists around you.

CHAPTER 6

Slow Your Roll (God's in Control)

'For my thoughts are not your thoughts, neither are your ways my ways,' declares the Lord. 'As the heavens are higher than the earth, so are my ways higher than your ways and my thoughts than your thoughts.'

Isaiah 55:8-9

When it comes to acknowledging life's challenges, there is one more thing to address if we are going to learn to truly enjoy life. We must recognize the fact that ultimately, we are simply not in control……of anything really.

For those of us who to some degree are "control-freaks" like me, that can be a hard truth to acknowledge. My control issues typically revolve around organization and administrative things. Just recently have I learned to not get super antsy, anxious, or even frustrated when things aren't planned out, down to the last detail. I even plan the details of my relaxation days. But, despite my efforts, there are always those instances where things are going to go not only slightly off track, but sometimes in an entirely different direction than what I was even aiming for.

Some of us try to control people. Whether it's by deception, lying, gossiping, discouragement, seduction, or brutality, we have to find a way to manipulate the situation so that people will act, say or think a certain way that we want them to. Some of us, especially in the Christian arena, have the "savior complex". We always have to be saving someone, from someone or something.

Whether we are trying to control people, our finances, our situations, our businesses, our homes, our churches, or the world we live in, we will always be limited in our own capabilities. Even with the best and most humble intentions, what we have planned is still nothing compared to what God has in store.

The header verse for this chapter, from Isaiah reminds us that our ways and thoughts are nowhere near God's ways and thoughts. He always sees the big picture! Not to mention the fact, that He is the author of life and already knows everything that He has deemed to occur.

We wear ourselves out so much trying to make an impact, effect change, motivate people toward a purpose, and push others to hit their goals. None of these are bad in and of themselves. However, where we fail and end up frustrated, discouraged, confused, and upset, is in our reactions when "our ways" don't get the results we want.

We forget that ultimately, God is in control of everything and everyone. No person changes unless God deems them to change. No circumstance or situation changes unless God deems it so.

It's true he uses us and others as vessels to effect the changes, but outside of that, we have no ultimate control.

It is so important to acknowledge this, so that we do not tirelessly waste our efforts, energy, time, and resources trying to control things that only God can. So, are we just supposed to stop trying to help people altogether? Nope. I promise, that is not at all what I'm saying.

You see, so often we try so hard to help others. Whether it's by giving advice, writing a recommendation letter for a job, letting their kids carpool with yours to school, loaning them money in times of need, letting them sleep on your couch for a night or two, keeping them from literally beating the crap out of someone, taking them to AA meetings, making sure they have a ride to bible study, being an accountability partner to keep them out of trouble, or even bailing them out of jail – these are all great gestures, and acts of love and kindness.

Sometimes these gestures are exactly what the recipient needs to keep them from making a bad choice, going off the deep end, ending up in prison, or even committing suicide. But sadly, there are other times, when these good gestures only yield *temporary* results that keep the recipient off the ledge for only a day or so. Then the next thing you know that same person does the exact opposite of what you advised them to do.

They take your money, spend it on something completely different from what they said it was for, and never pay you back. They start drinking again after 5 years of sobriety. They stop coming to bible study and church. They get fired after a week, from the job you helped them get. They bash their neighbor's head in and end up arrested.

Whatever the outcome may be, I am learning that in either scenario, **I am NOT God**. My responsibility is to do what God has called me as a Christian to do – show love, in whatever way I can. So many years, especially in ministry, I used to try to "fix" so many people, solve their problems, answer their prayers, and patch up their lives. In short, I tried to be God. Although, He definitely uses us a vessels to accomplish His will and influence others' lives, we have to remember that ultimately, He does the fixing, the changing, and the problem-solving in the world around us.

We shouldn't feel guilt, or pressure for that matter, to try and be God – not even for our family or closest friends.

I've even been guilty of changing my own personal goals and dreams just to allow myself to be a "savior" to others. God has recently taught me, that I should definitely help if and when I can, but that I should continue to walk in His plan for my own life in the process. The awesome thing about all this, is that when we do step aside. and allow God to work, time actually passes. Then you look back and see not only how God has worked in your own life but also in the life of the person you were originally trying to help.

It's even more amazing when you realize that God works things out much better than anything you could have done.   On the flip side, even if that person doesn't end up in a good place, you can sleep better knowing it's not your fault, or your place to go fix it, because God is in control of that too.

If we are going to truly enjoy the life Jesus died for us to have, we must learn to "slow our roll", and remember that God is in control! As cliche, as it may sound, do what you can to help, pray for others, and then let go, and let God!

Putting it into Practice

- ➢ Read and meditate on the verses below regarding God's attributes and sovereign power:
    - Proverbs 19:21
    - Psalm 24:1, 135:6-7
    - Isaiah 46:3-5, 64:8
    - Matthew 19:26
- ➢ What areas of your life right now are you trying to plan or control all on your own, and leaving God out in the process?
- ➢ What people have you been trying hard to have an impact on or help? Have you given God enough room to work in their lives, or in the situation?
- ➢ What situations or relationships have gone wrong that you are blaming yourself for not "fixing"? Is there anything that you can or should do to resolve it? Have you prayed about it and given it to God?
- ➢ Vow today to start asking God to direct you regarding control issues in your life. Over the next 30 days make a list of all the things you watch God do, as you step aside and let Him take control!

WARNING

Relinquishing control will be very hard at first, even scary for some. However, the following possible side effects will be well worth it: noticeable stress relief, less anxiety and frustration, decreased guilt, worry and doubt, ability to slow down and relax more often, and an enhanced prayer life.

NOTE: some people you used to try and "fix" may start calling you selfish, accuse you of not caring as much, or even stop talking to you, or being your friend. DO NOT let that trick or guilt you into going back and over-exerting your time, efforts, energy, and resources to attempt to "fix" them again.

Extended use of this product is guaranteed to produce answered prayers, blessings, joy, and peace – in your life and the lives of those around you!

SECTION III:

Check Your Emotions

"Like a city whose walls are broken through
is a person who lacks self-control."

Proverbs 25:28

As human beings, by nature, we are full of many emotions.   It is easy to allow those emotions to control us. However, as Christians, by the power of the Holy Spirit within us, we don't have to allow our emotions to reign free and dictate what we say, do, or even how we feel.

In this section, we will look at three key things that tend to hinder our walk with God, and our ability to enjoy life in Christ. If we learn to recognize these emotions and implement what the bible teaches us about them, we will then learn how to keep them in check. Then we can stop allowing how we feel, rob us of the joy God intended us to have.

CHAPTER 7

Get Rid of Worry

Can any one of you by worrying add a single hour to your life?

Matthew 6:27

Worry is one of those emotions that everyone grapples with from time to time. It is when we allow our mind to dwell on our difficulties and troubles. It is when we give way to anxiety, or unease over actual or even potential problems. And our enemy, the devil, preys heavily on us whenever we allow this emotion to reign in our lives.

About five years ago, God started to deal with me heavily on the topic of worry. I was getting more and more into writing for my blog, ministry with kids, and just growing in my walk with God. Just when I thought I was learning to talk to God more, and let my everyday problems, circumstances and issues just roll off my back, the devil tried a new tactic. He started getting me to worry about the future and stuff that *could* happen. I started to get plagued with "what if" thoughts out of the blue like:

- What if your truck breaks down for real this week? How are you going to get a new car?
- You don't want your son going to public school for middle school do you?
- How are you going to afford to send him to college when he turns 18?
- More and more family members are being diagnosed with cancer; what if you're next?
- What if your job starts laying off people? You haven't even begun to rebuild your savings back up yet.
- What if you die tomorrow? Did you revise your will? Is your life insurance current?

- What if something bad happens to mom or dad? How are you going to take care of them?

After these thoughts continued for a few weeks, effecting my mood, my conversation, and my day to day responsibilities, I realized what the enemy was trying to do. I was upset at myself for letting it go that long. Then I did what I already knew to do, but had momentarily forgotten, as Christians often do. I went to God in prayer and picked up His Word! And here is the exact passage He directed me to:

Matthew 6:25-34 (TLB): "So my counsel is: Don't worry about things—food, drink, and clothes. For you already have life and a body—and they are far more important than what to eat and wear. Look at the birds! They don't worry about what to eat—they don't need to sow or reap or store up food—for your heavenly Father feeds them. And you are far more valuable to him than they are. Will all your worries add a single moment to your life?

And why worry about your clothes? Look at the field lilies! They don't worry about theirs. Yet King Solomon in all his glory was not clothed as beautifully as they. And if God cares so wonderfully for flowers that are here today and gone tomorrow, won't he more surely care for you, O men of little faith? So don't worry at all about having enough food and clothing. Why be like the heathen? For they take pride in all these things and are deeply concerned about them. But your heavenly Father already knows perfectly well that you need them, and he will give them to you if you give him first place in your life and live as he wants you to.

So don't be anxious about tomorrow. God will take care of your tomorrow too. Live one day at a time."

What a refresher! And boy did I need that exact passage! The bottom line is, so often, the things we worry about are far beyond our control. In fact, we tend to worry about things that ONLY God can handle. We don't have to look far to find things in our lives that are wrong, broken, lacking, messed up, bad, or frustrating. But, if we stay focused on only those things, all the time, we will inevitably worry. In fact, our minds will actually inflate the situations to make them seem bigger than what they really are. And that turns into creating other worries for tomorrow, and the next day, and the next. To the point where we even worry about the far distant future. But, the passage clearly tells us to stop worrying about life, because God will take care of our today and our tomorrow.

Worrying never does us any good. In fact, it only makes what we are going through even worse.

Now before you ask, I'm not saying that we don't need to be *concerned* about some of the things that come up in our lives, or thoughts that pop up in our minds (such as those I listed). There are things that will happen that will need, and even demand our immediate attention. However, those things that we have absolutely no control over, those things we can't do anything to change – those are the things we absolutely must learn to entrust to God.

As mentioned in previous chapters, we all know life is a challenge and every day presents its own version of that challenge. However, the beauty of having a relationship with God, is that we don't have to go through life like those who don't have a relationship with Him. He has given us direct access to Himself for a purpose, and we can go to Him in prayer anytime. We also have His Word, so that He can speak to us anytime. When we utilize these two things together, there is nothing we can't handle.

So what it comes down to is this: Life is hard and will continue to be hard. But, in the midst of this life, we have a choice to make each day. We can take our concerns and turn them into worries, which will lead to stress, anxiety, anger, and coping mechanisms that will produce other issues. OR, we can take our concerns to God in prayer and leave them with Him to handle for us. After all, it's not like we can solve them on our own anyway.

I Peter 5:7 (TLB) says, "Let him have all your worries and cares, for He is always thinking about you and watching everything that concerns you". I know it's one of those things that is easier said than done. However, as Christians, if we do not learn to get rid of worry, we will continue to rob ourselves of enjoying the life God intended us to have. Trust me, by nature I am one of those people that like to have a plan for everything. It took me a very long time to not only learn what the bible said about worry, but to implement it, and start to relinquish the power of that emotion in my life.

Not worrying meant me not being in control. It meant taking a leap of faith. It meant trusting God even when it looked like no resolutions were in sight. But, do you know what the best part of getting rid of worry is? It allows room for God to work in your life. It allows us to see the power, love, and blessings of God in our lives.

These "mountains" that scare us, and cause us to worry and stress over and over, are nothing to God. Because there is nothing impossible for Him.

The devil is counting on us being fixated on the circumstances of life and therefore, being consumed with worry. He wants us to feel anxious and powerless, to experience sleepless nights, and to be robbed of joy and peace.

I guarantee, that once you begin to work on getting rid of worry, you will begin to experience immediate relief – physically, mentally, and spiritually. As Christians we must give God room to work. Don't allow your circumstances to get you worried to the point where you forget to lean on God, and end up missing His blessings, and not enjoying life.

Putting it into Practice

> ➢ Read and meditate on the verses below regarding worry (some were mentioned in this chapter):
>   - Matthew 6:25-34
>   - I Peter 5:7
>   - Philippians 4:6-7
>   - John 14:1
>   - Mark 13:11

➢ Begin by asking God to help you get rid of worry. This is not something that comes naturally, nor is it something that you can do on your own. Remember it will take time.

➢ Make a list of the things you have been worried about lately and why. Circle all the things on your list that you have no control over. Take time to pray about each of the circled items and verbally state that you are "handing them over to God". Then fold that paper up and stick it in the back of your bible. Set a reminder in your phone or on a calendar to revisit the list in 30 days.

➢ Take a mental note of every time you feel yourself worrying about something and pause to say a prayer to God in regards to whatever it is that you are worrying about.

➢ When your reminder comes up in 30 days, revisit your list and make a note of what God has done in your life since then. Then revise the list (adding any new worries and/or crossing off things that you no longer worry about). Pray and repeat the original process. The goal is that in time, your list should get shorter and shorter as you learn to "get rid of worry". Eventually, you won't need to keep making a list, as you will learn to recognize worry when you see it, and will pray and deal with it on the spot as it arises.

WARNING

Embarking on a mission to get rid of worry will seem difficult at first. However, the more you push through and stay dedicated to doing it, the more relief you will experience. Possible side effects include: fewer tension headaches, less frowning, a more relaxed demeanor and attitude, a huge reduction in stress, less crying, and a decrease in emotional outbursts.

NOTE: other people who tend to worry frequently will not want to be around you as much, because your newfound attitude of "not worrying" will annoy them.   Likewise, their constant worrying will begin to annoy you.

Extended use of this product is guaranteed to build your faith and trust in God. You will also feel much better overall, and the lack of worrying will be evident in your appearance and facial expressions.

44

CHAPTER 8

Control Your Anger

*In your anger do not sin. Do not let the sun go down
while you are still angry.*

Ephesians 4:26

In today's present age, there is no shortage of angry people. They are all around us. People are angry about their job, their spouse, their kids, their finances, their car, the weather, traffic, their coffee, what their best friend said, their teacher, their neighbor, their dog, their lives. Our society is simply full of angry people. And that includes you and I. In fact, if we're being honest, sometimes we even get angry with God.

Anger, as an emotion, is not wrong in and of itself. In fact, there are, and will be many occasions which warrant us being angry. The problem is we allow our anger, whether warranted or not, to lead to bigger issues.

The verse above from Ephesians 4:26 doesn't tell us NOT to be angry. It tells us not to *sin* when we get angry. In other words, don't allow whatever or whomever has pissed you off to the point of boiling anger, cause you to go out and do something that isn't right. So, no! Seeking revenge, taking matters into your own hands, harming someone, spreading rumors and lies, or breaking the law, is not the proper response.

And if you're a smart-aleck Christian like me, you may be saying, ok, I won't go out and do anything in sin. I'll just sit and be angry instead because it feels good. Welp newsflash: staying angry and just letting the anger fester is wrong too. The second part of that same verse tells us not to let the sun go down while we're still angry. In other words, we should deal with our anger, and deal with it quickly.

Take a few minutes to reflect on something or someone that has made you angry recently. Now reflect on how you handled that anger. When it happened how long did you think about the situation? How many people did you call or text about it? How did it effect the rest of your day or week? What was your emotional response? Did you cuss, cry, scream, yell, or punch someone? Did you storm out of the room or house? Did you get the situation resolved? Are you still angry about it?

It is not hard to see how much we can lose out on by not dealing with our anger and learning to control it.   Anger can rob us of our joy, peace, time, relationships, and many other things.   Sometimes without even realizing it, we even harbor unresolved anger from our past.

You know when you see a person you haven't seen in a really long time. Yet, at the sight of them all the anger just comes rushing back as if the original situation just happened all over again. How about when someone we are currently dating does something to remind us of an ex, and we snap out of the blue because we are still angry from the previous relationship. How about when one of your close friends asks you for a favor, but you snap and bring up that time you did something for them three years ago where they never paid you back.

Sometimes we even get angry about things that haven't happened yet. We let negative thinking and influence get us stirred up about what we think *could* happen to us.

- You're applying for a better position within the same company, but don't believe you're as qualified as your co-worker Lisa who also applied. So, for the next week, while waiting for a decision to be made, you're angry at Lisa and your boss.
- Your son fails one math test. You feel like you've failed as a parent. Now for the next month, you're angry at your son because you feel he's going to fail 8th grade completely.
- Your father left your mother when you were younger. Ever since you have just been angry and resentful to any male that crosses your path.

James 1:19-20 says, "My dear brothers and sisters, take note of this: Everyone should be quick to listen, slow to speak and slow to become angry, because human anger does not produce the righteousness that God desires." These verses teach that not only should we work on controlling what we do when we get angry, but that we should work on not getting angry in the first place! This is why it is so important for us to take a close look at what it is that angers us. What people, places, conversations, or things tend to trigger our anger? Once we determine our triggers, then we can focus on *why* we let those specific things trigger our anger. And then we can work on ways to deal with and control our anger.

Some people may genuinely have deeply rooted issues at the heart of their anger that requires professional intervention or therapy. Even if you fall into that category, the good news is that all Christians have the power of the Holy Spirit within them to gain control over anger.

The bible equates a person who learns to control their anger with one who is wise, and the person who is constantly angry as a fool:

Proverbs 29:8 – "Mockers stir up a city, but the wise turn away anger."

Ecclesiastes 7:9 – "Do not be quickly provoked in your spirit, for anger resides in the lap of fools."

In the book of Genesis, God looked at Abel's offering with favor, but did not do so regarding the offering from his brother Cain. If you know the story, Cain did not take this too well:

Genesis 4:6-7 – "Then the LORD said to Cain, 'Why are you angry? Why is your face downcast? If you do what is right, will you not be accepted? But if you do not do what is right, sin is crouching at your door; it desires to have you, but you must rule over it'."

Here we have a classic example of getting angry when things don't go our way; even when it's our own fault! In fact, after God makes the statement above to Cain, he goes on to lure his brother out into the field, only to kill him. Talk about allowing anger to fester and cause you to sin! This is why the bible warns us to get our anger under control. If we don't, it is inevitable that it will lead us to do things that don't please God.

Proverbs 29:22 – "An angry person stirs up conflict, and a hot-tempered person commits many sins."

Psalms 37:8 – "Refrain from anger and turn from wrath; do not fret—it leads only to evil."

Think about all the emotion and energy that goes into being angry. It literally changes our entire demeanor and can effect our bodies in different ways. From a physical perspective, both short and long term anger have been known to cause headaches, digestion problems, abdominal pain, insomnia, increased anxiety, depression, high blood pressure, skin problems, heart attacks and strokes.

As for coping mechanisms, sometimes it requires us to be proactive and take certain steps to deal with our anger:

- Take a walk
- Go to the gym
- Literally walk away (get out of the environment or presence of the person you are angry with)
- Deep breathing exercises
- Listen to music
- Seek help if necessary – whether speaking with a trusted confidante or a professional

The devil wants us to be angry as much as possible because he knows that uncontrolled anger leads to sin.

So he will put anything and anyone he can in your path to provoke you to anger and keep you angry. Sadly, as stated previously, the devil really doesn't have to put forth much effort these days in the anger department. Christians are walking around just as angry as everyone else.

The key to dealing with anger (just like everything else in this book), is spending time reading God's Word on the subject. Once you do that and recognize anger for what it really is, you begin to truly see why God wants us to work on not allowing it to control us. There is no way we will truly enjoy life the way He intended if we harbor so much anger inside.

I can make a list of things that I know triggers my anger in general. I can also name a few things or people from my past that I still harbor towards. However, I am so grateful that God has been slowly but steadily working in my life to help me deal with and control my anger. I was a typical "angry black woman" for many years of my Christian life. People around me didn't necessarily know it, or even see it. But I knew it, and felt it. I was miserable inside.

Dealing with anger is so liberating. When you begin to get to that place where the things people do or say just don't effect you the way they used to – it feels amazing! When circumstances that used to set you off in a fit of rage don't even bother you anymore – its awesome!

Now I want to be completely clear – dealing with your anger is not suppressing it or pretending that it isn't there. We don't want to harbor anger just for it to explode down the road. We want to identify anger, it's triggers, and the reasons behind it, so we can work to resolve it. That resolution process can take time, especially if other people are involved, or if professional help is required. However, I encourage you to remember that you can't control other people. In other words, the person who is the root cause of your anger may not change. So in that case, you may need to take steps to change your environment, or even end a toxic relationship.

We can only deal with our own anger. We are not responsible for the anger management of others.

I also want to point out that as Christians, we should not aim to be a source of anger for someone. There are several verses that talk about not provoking one another, but rather edifying one another and lifting each other up. We don't need to create ways to get people angry! In fact, we should attempt to de-escalate a situation if and when it is in our capability, or power to do so:

Proverbs 15:1 – "A gentle answer turns away wrath, but a harsh word stirs up anger."

If you're reading this and thinking 'I don't have any anger issues', then I say, dig deeper. Anger may not be a big issue for you, but I guarantee, it is worth addressing. Even if it's some minor thing, identify it, determine the trigger and deal with it. Holding on to it is stealing a portion of your joy.

Last time I checked, this book is all about learning to enjoy the life Jesus died for us to have. So why not make it your mission to get rid of and deal with anything standing in your way of doing that. Afterall, God has blessed us way too much for us to live in anger daily.

<u>*Putting it into Practice*</u>

- Take some time to really reflect and make a list of the things and people that make you angry (whether past or present). If you're having a hard time with this, monitor yourself for a few days and take note of each time you get angry and what triggered it.
- Next to each item on your list identify *why* it triggers your anger.
- Under those items list your current coping mechanisms. Put an "x" next to all those that are not beneficial or make matters worse (i.e. drinking, smoking, sex, etc.)
- Revisit the list of coping mechanisms mentioned in this chapter and list those that you could incorporate.
- Write out all of the verses referenced in this chapter. Begin to meditate on those verses daily.
- Ask God to help you deal with your anger. In your prayer time, be specific and use your list as a reference. Name the things that make you angry and commit them to God.
- Remember, dealing with anger doesn't happen overnight. It will take time. But, with God all things are possible!
- PLEASE seek professional help if your anger is completely out of control! Don't be afraid to admit it. That is the first step to recovery.

WARNING

Learning to control your anger will not only seem difficult, but your flesh will naturally be opposed to it. The non-Christian world around us will contradict this concept on many levels. However, dedication to this cause will prove to be worth it on a spiritual, physical, and mental level. Possible side effects include: joy, inner peace, frequent smiles, low stress levels, and an overall attitude of just not caring what people say, think or do.

NOTE: The less angry you become in general, the more others will tend to get angry with you.

The more you use this product, the more you will develop an emotional allergy to angry people and will want to avoid being in their presence altogether.

CHAPTER 9

Stop Dwelling on Past Mistakes

Forget the former things; do not dwell on the past.

Isaiah 43:18

Another thing that weighs on us emotionally and hinders us from enjoying life, is the fact that we tend to dwell on our past mistakes. As Christians, we can quote all the verses that talk about how "forgiven" we are, and the fact that we are no longer condemned because of our sins. However, so many of us still struggle with forgiving ourselves and moving on from things we have done in the past. We have to stop allowing our minds and the devil to deceive us into thinking that God can't use us because of our past mistakes or sins.

The first step to being able to do this, is to not only read or know what Scripture says on this topic, but to truly embrace its truths.

Truth #1: We MUST know who we are in Christ and realize that our relationship with Him completely changes our standing in regards to sin.

- I Corinthians 5:17 – "Therefore, if anyone is in Christ, the new creation has come. The old has gone, the new is here!"
- Romans 8:1 – "Therefore, there is now no condemnation for those who are in Christ Jesus."
- I John 1:9 – "If we confess our sins, he is faithful and just and will forgive us our sins and purify us from all unrighteousness."
- Romans 8:38-39 – "For I am convinced that neither death nor life, neither angels nor demons, neither the present nor the future, nor any powers, neither height nor depth, nor anything else in all creation, will be able to separate us from the love of God that is in Christ Jesus our Lord."

These verses plainly tell us that once we accept Jesus as our Lord and Savior and give our lives to Him that we are literally like new! We are no longer condemned to die and go to hell for our sins.   And any sins we commit going forward can and will be forgiven as well. In fact, nothing we have done, are doing, or will do, as Christians, can ever separate us from the love of God!

The quicker we acknowledge and embrace this truth, the easier it will be for us to stop dwelling on the things we have done in our past.

Truth #2: Christianity is a life-long process!

- Philippians 1:6 (NLT) – "And I am certain that God, who began the good work within you, will continue his work until it is finally finished on the day when Christ Jesus returns."
- Philippians 3:13-14 (NLT) – "No, dear brothers and sisters, I have not achieved it, but I focus on this one thing: Forgetting the past and looking forward to what lies ahead, I press on to reach the end of the race and receive the heavenly prize for which God, through Christ Jesus is calling us."

Through His Holy Spirit that lives within us, God is constantly working on us to be more and more "Christ-like". And He will continue to do so amongst all Christians until the day Jesus returns!

Likewise, as the Apostle Paul said in Philippians 3:13-14, we should have an attitude of striving to be more Christ-like. No, we should not dwell on past sins and mistakes. However, we also should not keep making the same mistakes and committing the same sins over and over either. Our attitude should be that of someone who is "pressing forward for the prize" in this Christian race of life. The goal has to be to continue to get better; to become more Christ-like.

Truth #3: All the great "heroes" of the bible were used by God in spite of their past sins!

Just to name a few:
- Abraham – the liar
- Moses – the murderer

- Jacob – the deceiver
- Rahab – the prostitute
- David – the adulterer
- Peter – denied knowing Christ
- Paul – the persecutor of the church

If God used all these men and women in the capacity that he did, despite the mistakes they made in their past, then it sounds to me like we all pass the eligibility test!

In fact, the more you read through the bible, you will see that God often used those with "troubling pasts" to do great and mighty things for His namesake.

Isaiah 43:18-19 says, "Forget the former things; do not dwell on the past. See, I am doing a new thing! Now it springs up; do you not perceive it? I am making a way in the wilderness and streams in the wasteland." The thing we have to always remember, is that God already knows everything there is to know about us (past, present, and future). Nothing takes Him by surprise, and nothing can thwart His plan for our lives. Surely no past mistake or sin is capable of messing with the destiny that God Has in store for us. That verse is such an awesome reminder and encouragement that God is always doing something new in our lives – no matter what!

So stop dwelling on your past mistakes! It does you no good, and it does the people around you no good. And as you can see, biblically it is not something God wants us doing anyway.

Sometimes, even if you have moved on from the past, the devil will often use those close to you to bring up old things to try and use against you. Or, maybe your current situation is a result of some past mistake, and you are literally reminded about it daily because it stares you right in the face. Either way, the same truths mentioned in this chapter apply. Whatever the case may be, we must move forward and stop looking back. The only way to truly be equipped to do so, is to constantly, saturate our minds with the truths of God's Word. Isn't it funny how everything comes back to spending more time with God's Word.

So you want to enjoy your life more? Then you absolutely MUST stop dwelling on your past mistakes. Trust me, continuing to do so, will only continue to hinder your spiritual growth and cause you to miss out on the fullness of joy God intended you to have. Instead of dwelling on the bad or negative aspects of your past, use your past as a reference point to measure your growth. Let your present be a testimony of where God has brought you from, and where He is taking you!

Putting it into Practice

➢ What past mistakes have you been dwelling on? Why?

➢ Begin to meditate on the verses mentioned in this chapter daily.

➢ Pick at least one character mentioned under Truth #2 and look up their full story in the bible.

➢ Ask God to help you to stop dwelling on your past mistakes. Ask Him to help you forgive yourself if necessary.

➢ Make a commitment to move forward by focusing on who you are in Christ, spending more time in God's Word, and striving to become more Christlike by the power of the Holy Spirit within you.

➢ Keep a journal of the changes and new things you start to see God doing in your life!

WARNING

When you stop dwelling on your past mistakes, you can almost always expect others to start reminding you about them instead. So don't be surprised if and when it happens. Don't let them deter you! God will begin to do new things in your life and those same people may try to discourage your progress when they see it happening.

NOTE: Use of this product will cause you to feel liberated and joyful! It may even feel like a huge burden(s) has been lifted off your shoulders. Just go with it and begin to enjoy life more!

SECTION IV:

Remember Self-Care

No one hates his own body but feeds and cares for it,
just as Christ cares for the church.

Ephesians 5:29 (NLT)

Believe it or not, some Christians tend to think that self-care is unnecessary or selfish. After all, if the bible says God will supply all of our needs (Philippians 4:19), and that we should look on the interest of others more than our own (Philippians 2:4), then why should we even be entertaining the thought of self-care?

However, I promise you, that there is no way we can neglect self-care, and still enjoy life the way God intended.

CHAPTER 10

Take Care of Your Body

Do you not know that your bodies are temples of the Holy Spirit, who is in you, whom you have received from God? You are not your own; you were bought at a price. Therefore honor God with your bodies.

I Corinthians 6:19-20

When it comes to talking about taking care of our body, it is so important to start with recognizing how much of a miracle every human being truly is. In the story of creation, God literally *spoke* everything into existence.

Genesis 1:3 – "And God said, 'Let there be light,' and there was light."

This same pattern went on for the first five days of creation, with God simply speaking everything into existence (water, skies, birds, animals, land, plants, creatures, etc.). Ah, but on day six, when it came to the creation of man, God himself put in some work!

Genesis 1:26-27 – "Then God said, 'Let us **make** mankind in our image'………So God **created** mankind in his own image."

Genesis 2:7 – "Then the Lord God **formed** a man from the dust of the ground and **breathed into his nostrils** the breath of life and the man became a living being."

And everyone else, including you and I, that has existed since the creation of the first man, continues to be a replica of God's divine handiwork.

Psalms 139:13-14 – "For you created my inmost being; you knit me together in my mother's womb. I praise you because I am fearfully and wonderfully made; your works are wonderful, I know that full well."

Once we realize the miracle that our bodies truly are, then we can begin to appreciate it from a spiritual perspective. Let's look deeper into the scripture used at the heading of this chapter.

> I Corinthians 6:19-20 – "Do you not know that **your bodies are temples of the Holy Spirit**, who is in you, whom you have received from God? **You are not your own; you were bought at a price**. Therefore **honor God with your bodies**."

Key Points:

- As Christians, our bodies are temples of the Holy Spirit who lives in us.
- We are not our own, as Jesus sacrificed himself for us to truly live, and we belong to God.
- Because of this, we should honor God by properly taking care of our bodies.

Now if you read the full context of these verses, you will see that the Apostle Paul was speaking specifically on the topic of sexual immorality, and reminding the saints in the church of Corinth that they should be keeping themselves pure and honoring God with their bodies. However, that is not the only reason, or way in which God wants us to honor Him with our bodies.

So what exactly does the bible say about taking care of these miraculous temples in which His Spirit dwells? I'm glad you asked! It comes down to three basic things we know we should do, but now we'll have a biblical basis for why we do them.

A Healthy Diet

Now I'm not writing to preach on healthy eating or the top ten diets. In fact, *healthy diet* is a relative term. From a biblical perspective, I've got three points on this topic:

- **Eat!**

Ephesians 5:29 (NLT) says, "No one hates his own body but feeds and cares for it, just as Christ cares for the church."
Starving ourselves is out of the question! We must eat in order to properly nourish our bodies. Please note that this does not include fasting, which is a completely separate topic for another book.

- **But, watch what you eat!**

I Corinthians 10:31 says. "So whether you eat or drink or whatever you do, do it all for the glory of God." Although personally, I am an advocate for healthy eating, I won't give you a list of things that I think you should eat and not eat. Instead I encourage you to *think* about what you're eating regularly.

If whatever we eat or drink should glorify God, ask yourself 'is my current diet causing me to be overweight, sick, sluggish, weak, unfocused, and unhealthy? How is it effecting my temple and the work that God has called me to do?'

- **Stop overindulging! Period!**

I will quote two proverbs regarding this matter:

Proverbs 23:20-21 – "Do not join those who drink too much wine or gorge themselves on meat, for drunkards and gluttons become poor, and drowsiness clothes them in rags."

Proverbs 25:16 – "If you find honey, eat just enough – too much of it, and you will vomit."

Simply put, moderation is always key, no matter what your diet is. Think of how you feel when you overeat, overindulge, or get drunk. Unless you enjoy feeling miserable, simply practicing moderation is an easy way to work on your diet. Plus, you'll feel better and be more effective!

Stay Active / Exercise

Don't worry. I'm not here to preach or dictate a physical fitness routine for you either. In fact, the bible teaches the importance of spiritual exercise and growing in faith more so than physical exercise.

I Timothy 4:8 – "For physical training is of some value, but godliness has value for all things, holding promise for both the present life and the life to come."

Now don't mis-interpret this to mean you should focus on spiritual growth *only* and negate physical fitness altogether. The verse says that physical training does have *some* value. And the bible also has A LOT to say about laziness. The basic definition of lazy is unwillingness to work or use energy. I won't quote all the verses here, just a select few:

Proverbs 13:4 (NLT) – "Lazy people want much but get little, but those who work hard will prosper."

Proverbs 21:25 (NLT) – "Despite their desires, the lazy will come to ruin, for their hands refuse to work."

Romans 12:11 (NLT) – "Never be lazy, but work hard and serve the Lord enthusiastically."

At the very least, we should be active. Move! Do something! Whether you hit the gym or not, its clear that as Christians, God never intended for us to be lazy. *How* you stay active is up to you. However, I'm a witness that when it comes to taking care of your body, staying active and exercising does wonders for your energy levels and your emotional well-being. Plus, you just feel better overall.

Proper Rest

This is a big one many people overlook. Especially those of us with many responsibilities. Some days between work, ministry, family, hobbies, and life in general, we find ourselves constantly on the go. We push ourselves so hard, and get very little rest. We don't allow our bodies to recuperate. So, we are always tired, or feeling exhausted and worn out.

Psalms 127:2 (NLT) – "It is useless for you to work so hard from early morning until late at night, anxiously working for food to eat; for God gives rest to his loved ones."

Mark 6:31 (NLT) – "Then Jesus said, 'Let's go off by ourselves to a quiet place and rest awhile.' He said this because there were so many people coming and going that Jesus and his apostles didn't even have time to eat."

God wants us to have proper rest daily. Rest is important for recuperation and restoration of our bodies. We all know there is nothing like a good night's sleep! Or even a mid-day nap.

Being a person who suffers from insomnia every now and then, it is never fun to even try to run on fumes. Despite what the hecticness of our society may dictate to us, we need to get proper rest daily. As you can see in the verse above from Mark, even when it comes to "doing the work of the Lord", we can't just keep going and going and going like the Energizer bunny. Even Jesus rested!

The bottom line is, we need to take care of our bodies – they are the vessels that God has blessed us with. Temples of the Holy Spirit within us.

If we don't eat right, stay active, or get proper rest, we will feel miserable, burnout, and may even face unnecessary health issues. Most importantly, we will be less effective for God, and we certainly won't enjoy life the way He intended.

Putting it into Practice

➢ On a scale of 1-10 (with 10 being the highest), how would you rate your overall physical health? How do you typically feel each day?

- ➤ What things from your diet do you need to work on, as far as, moderation? What things do you need to get rid of completely?
- ➤ How active are you on a weekly basis? Do you make it a point to move around when you can, take a walk, or exercise? Or would you consider yourself lazy?
- ➤ How much sleep do you get daily? Are you constantly tired or feeling worn out?
- ➤ Knowing that your body is a temple for God, what commitment(s) are you going to make to Him to start taking better care of it? Make a list!
- ➤ Commit your list to prayer. Just like everything else in this book, you can't do it alone. Ask God to give you strength and willingness to do what you need to do to properly take care of His temple. Ask Him to help you not to be lazy.

WARNING

Diligently working to take care of your body will have your energy levels at an all time high. You will begin to look, feel and sound so much better. Continued use of the is product will cause your dependence on caffeine, energy drinks, medication, alcohol, and other social substances to lessen over time.

Don't be surprised if people start to wonder or ask "what's new with you". They will want your newfound sense of joy that results from you taking care of yourself, but few will be willing to do what you did to get there (that includes Christians and non-Christians alike).

CHAPTER 11

Guard Your Mind

Don't copy the behavior and customs of this world, but let God transform
you into a new person by changing the way you think.
Then you will learn to know God's will for you,
which is good and pleasing and perfect.

Romans 12:2 (NLT)

One of my favorite books of all time is *Battlefield of the Mind* by Joyce Meyer. It has been one of the most influential books for me regarding my Christian journey. It taught me to "think about what I'm thinking about". In other words, as Christians, we have to pay attention to what is going on inside our heads.

There are plenty of negative influences all around us that seek to keep our minds set and focused on all the wrong things. Just looking at the news alone, will be enough to get you depressed. There is no shortage of negative, awful, nerve-racking things going on in society. Not to mention temptations of the flesh, and the allure of sin everywhere on TV, the internet, and social media.

If we are not careful, we can easily start to develop and copy the behavior and customs of the world as stated in the verse above. Which is exactly what God does NOT want us to do. So how exactly are we supposed to guard our minds in the midst of all this?

Our sanctification (the process of becoming more like Christ) starts with a transformation of our minds; a renewed way of thinking. When we first come to accept Christ as our Lord and Savior, we come with so much mental baggage. And depending on how old you were at the point of salvation, it could be an entire lifetime worth of stuff. We had a completely different way of life before we came to know Christ. Our views, our thoughts, our words, our habits, our beliefs, our philosophy, our entire being – was different!

Transforming all that is a process, and it's not one that we get through on our own. In fact, the only way for our minds to be transformed – you guessed it – is by the power of the Holy Spirit within in us, and by spending more and more time reading God's Word!

Colossians 3:2 says, "Set your minds on things above, not on earthly things." The more time we spend reading and learning God's Word, the more God changes our minds from how we used to think, and the more He keeps us from adapting the non-Christian values, principles and belief systems of the world in which we live. And over time, we become more Christlike as we begin to know God's will for us.

The problem is, that it's so easy to conform to the thought process and beliefs of the non-Christian world around us. Whether its temptation from the devil, life's daily challenges, or other things beyond our control, it's easy to respond to things in a non-Christian way. Instead of checking our emotions as discussed in the previous section of this book, it is much easier to just keep worrying, stay angry, and keep dwelling on the past.

Unfortunately, we can't control every single thought that pops up in our mind. However, we can choose what to do with those thoughts once they show up. We can choose which thoughts to entertain or disregard.

We can choose when and how to shift our minds to other things, when our thinking begins to drift off track. The bible even tells us what types of things we *should* focus our minds on:

Philippians 4:8 – "Finally, brothers and sisters, whatever is true, whatever is noble, whatever is right, whatever is pure, whatever is lovely, whatever is admirable – if anything is excellent or praiseworthy – think about such things."

The best way to fill our minds with these type things that please God is to learn to saturate ourselves with God's Word.

Isaiah 26:3 (NLT) – "You will keep in perfect peace all who trust in you, all whose thoughts are fixed on you!"

The more we read God's Word, the more God's Word will infiltrate our daily thoughts, and the more peace we will have!

So how do we guard our minds?

- By spending more time reading God's Word
- By monitoring our thoughts so that we can discern good thinking from bad thinking
- By asking God for strength to shift our line of thinking to things that are pleasing to Him

Please don't take this lightly. In fact, I guarantee you that once you start to make a conscious effort to actually monitor your thoughts, you will be surprised at some of the things that go through your head. You will be even more surprised at the thoughts that linger. Whether its thoughts of jealousy, bitterness, rage, selfishness, revenge, low self-esteem, hatred, pride, violence, stubbornness, or perversion, trust me everyone has them.

Matthew 15:9 – "For out of the heart come evil thoughts – murder, adultery, sexual immorality, theft, false testimony, slander."

This is why, as Christians, we are called to undergo a transformation of our way of thinking to align with that of Christ. And in order to get there, we must actively work on guarding our minds daily.

Proverbs 23:7 (AMP) – "For as he thinks in his heart, so is he."

Everything we do and say, our emotions, our reactions, our facial expressions – all stem from what is going on inside of us. Allowing our thoughts to just run freely is not only displeasing to God, but it also hinders us from fully enjoying life the way God intended. If our thoughts are all over the place, and we are boggled down with the worries, stress, and anxieties of life all the time, that is the complete opposite of what God wants for us.

He wants us to spend more time in His Word, so we can learn to guard our thoughts, live in peace, and enjoy life. Why would we not want that for ourselves as well? Let's make a decision to feed our mind with the right things. It will require prayer and readiness to fight, because the mind truly is a battlefield – an ongoing, daily battle with your flesh, the devil, and the carnal influences of this world. But, with God we can successfully guard our minds and enjoy life more!

Putting it into Practice

- ➢ Take a day or two and monitor your thoughts. Try to make a list of the random things that pop into your head.
  NOTE: you won't be able to capture them all, but try to grab as many as you can.
- ➢ Analyze your list. Overall, what do you tend to think about most? What thoughts tend to linger? What is the percentage of good thoughts vs. bad thoughts?
- ➢ How often do you find yourself thinking on God, things He has spoken to you about from His Word, ministry, or what He has called you to do?
- ➢ Read and meditate on Philippians 4:8. Then make a list of things that fit into those categories of things the bible says we should think about.
- ➢ Begin to pray and ask God to help you shift your thoughts to things that are pleasing to Him.

WARNING

Learning to guard your mind, will severely shift things in your life. Things that you used to obsess over, or that drove you crazy will begin to cease to be a factor. You will begin to look at people, things, and life around you a completely different way.

Beware that the devil will NOT like this change you are making, and he will do everything he can to keep your thoughts and mind focused on things of this world, rather than on what pleases God. Don't be surprised if temptations and distractions seem to increase around you, to steer you off track!

CHAPTER 12

Work on Self-Discipline

For the Spirit God gave us does not make us timid, but gives us power, love, and self-discipline.

II Timothy 1:7

The pursuit of self-discipline has been a seemingly lost art among the masses, regardless of what point in history we find ourselves in. It's one of those things that most will only work towards periodically. And then …… well, most just quit and give up.

As Christians, we don't have the luxury of having the attitude that our non-Christian counterparts do when it comes to a lack of self-discipline. We can't just say 'this is how I am' and keep it moving. When we give our lives to God, His Holy Spirit comes to dwell in us, and we receive divine power, and help from above to do things that we couldn't do otherwise. According to the verse above, that includes self-discipline. In fact, as we grow in our walk with God, there are several *fruits* that we will begin to exhibit as Christians:

> Galatians 5:22-23 – "But the fruit of the Spirit is love, joy, peace, forbearance, kindness, goodness, faithfulness, gentleness and **self-control**."

Like with everything else God calls us to do, we don't just magically become self-disciplined people overnight. It is a learning process. The good news is that, as we continue to learn more of God's Word, the more He equips us to do the things he requires.

> II Peter 1:3 – "His divine power has given us everything we need for a godly life **through our knowledge of him** who called us by his own glory and goodness."

The Apostle Paul tells us that he *learned* to be disciplined, by the power of the Holy Spirit:

> Philippians 4:12-13 – "I know what it is to be in need, and I know what it is to have plenty. I have **learned** the secret of being content in any and every situation, whether well fed or hungry, whether living in plenty or in want. I can do all this through him who gives me strength."

We sometimes have the mindset that we can do things on our own, and only bring God in if our way fails. But the truth is, things tend to fail because we try to do them without God.

By doing things without God we actually set ourselves up to fail, or at the very least, we set ourselves up to take the longer road to success. In order to enjoy life the way God intended, we have to learn to work on self-discipline. No matter what area of your life you need it most – dieting, exercising, finances, relationships, studying, a new business venture, or even your walk with God – there is no way around self-discipline. Let's look at some specifics from the bible.

Self-Discipline Never Includes Procrastination

We've all heard the saying that procrastination is the thief of time. And time is the one thing we can never get back once it's gone. Procrastination not only hinders our progress, but sometimes we allow it to stop our success in certain areas altogether. We literally put off some things, and then forget about them.

> Proverbs 14:23 – "All hard work brings a profit, but mere talk leads only to poverty."

> Proverbs 27:1 – "Do not boast about tomorrow, for you do not know what a day may bring."

> Ephesians 5:15-16 – "Be very careful, then, how you live, not as unwise but as wise, making the most of every opportunity, because

the days are evil."

Everyone wants to hold off for tomorrow. We plan and live as if we are God and know that tomorrow is guaranteed. We act as if tomorrow we'll have more zeal than we do in the current moment. When in fact, we may never *feel* like doing certain things.

Self-discipline is not built on how we feel at all. Self-discipline is doing what needs to be done, everyday, regardless of how you feel.

The more we stop procrastinating and keep moving forward to do the things God has called us to do, the benefits are endless!

Self-Discipline Always Requires Hard Work

Yes. Hard work. The one thing we all try to avoid at some point or another. I love how Christians sometimes have the mentality that because we are Christians, we won't have to work as hard as others to accomplish things in life, because we have God. But, God did not give us a pass on hard work. He gave us His Holy Spirit to help us do the work, so that it wouldn't seem as hard.

Our hard work doesn't have to come with stress, anxiety, doubt, worry, fear and frustration. Yes, we will work our butts off. However, we can do it with hope, peace, joy, and strength, because God is with us. Below is one of my favorite passages of Scripture, which depicts a great imagery of what true *spiritual* self-discipline is:

I Corinthians 9:24-27 – "Do you not know that in a race all the runners run, but only one gets the prize? Run in such a way as to get the prize. Everyone who competes in the games goes into strict training. They do it to get a crown that will not last, but we do it to get a crown that will last forever. Therefore I do not run like someone running aimlessly; I do not fight like a boxer beating the air. No, I strike a blow to my body and make it my slave so that after I have preached to others, I myself will not be disqualified for the prize."

As you can see, a self-disciplined Christian is never in the race, just to be there. They are always in it to compete for the goal or prize. They go into strict training because they are working ultimately for God! They are tough on themselves and beat their bodies into subjection. Meaning they don't give in to temptations, impulses, or fleshly desires. They don't easily give up or quit.

Self-Discipline Requires You to Get Rid of Some Bad Habits

In order to develop self-discipline, sometimes we have to challenge ourselves to a make-over. A make-over in the sense of breaking a few bad habits in order to be successful in certain areas. Even when it comes to spiritual self-discipline, the bible names several things (bad habits) we must get rid of:

Colossians 3:5-8 – "Put to death, therefore, whatever belongs to your earthly nature: sexual immorality, impurity, lust, evil desires and greed, which is idolatry. Because of these, the wrath of God is coming. You used to walk in these ways, in the life you once lived. But now you must also rid yourselves of all such things as these: anger, rage, malice, slander, and filthy language from your lips."

We all have bad habits in one shape or form: always being late, smoking or drinking to deal with stress, overeating, not getting enough sleep, watching too much TV, using credit cards for everything, not paying people back what you owe, not finishing projects, using excessive foul language, always complaining, or gossiping. And of course, there are a thousand other things that could go on the list.

The Word of God teaches that because of Christ, we don't have to let our flesh (our emotions and feelings) control us. There is no bad habit that with the power of the Holy Spirit we can't beat if we make the decision to.

As Christians, let's stop making excuses, and stop letting society convince us into thinking we cannot be self-disciplined.

Remember it will take time for everyone – no exceptions! In fact, failure is guaranteed to be a part of the process. But guess what? When you slip, stumble or fall, it won't change the fact that you *can* do it, through Christ who gives you strength. It just means you have to keep relying on him along the way, and clinging to God's Word for guidance.

Let's stop being defeated, unmotivated, undisciplined Christians. God has given us the power to develop self-discipline, and make positive and productive changes in every area of our lives. I don't know about you, but I plan to tap into that power, and learn more and more of God's Word every day to guarantee my success, and therefore enjoy my life even more! The question is, how bad do you want it?

<u>Putting it into Practice</u>

- ➢ What areas of your life do you need some self-discipline in?
- ➢ What have you been procrastinating about?
- ➢ What bad habits do you need to break?
- ➢ Write down your top 3 areas that you want to focus on, as far as, self-discipline. Find verses in the bible that relate to those areas that you can meditate on daily and pray and commit them to God for help.
- ➢ Give yourself 30 days and record your progress along the way.

WARNING

When first utilizing this product you will notice several side effects up front, including, but not limited to: frustration, your body wanting to give up after the first few tries, tiredness, lack of zeal, negative thoughts, and an increase in distractions and temptations.   However, if you can push through all that, I guarantee it will be worth it!

Once you use this product in one area of your life, you will want to use it in other areas.   DO NOT brag to others about use of this product. Let the results speak for themselves.   Continued and excessive use will no doubt produce "haters". Don't let them deter you at all. Keep pressing forward and watch God do great things in all the areas of your life you apply this in!

SECTION V:

Nourish Your Relationships

Do to others as you would have them do to you.

Luke 6:31

A big part of enjoying life has to do with nourishing the relationships with those around you. For someone who is an introvert by nature, nourishing relationships does not come easy for me. In fact, I am often okay with not being around people at all (like 85 percent of the time).

However, God's plans are different and better than any we have. And very often He intends for us to be around people, if nothing more than to show Himself through what we say, and how we act. Even if it may not seem like it, working on our relationships with people in general is not only something we should do out of obedience to God, but it also results in a sense of joy that we won't obtain otherwise.

CHAPTER 13

Prioritize Family Time

*Don't look out only for your own interests, but take an interest
in others too. You must have the same attitude
that Christ Jesus had.*

Philippians 2:4-5 (NLT)

If there is one thing we as Christians should be constantly learning, its obedience to God. The world in which we live has its own philosophies and ways of doing things. One good thing to get into the habit of doing is constantly asking yourself, 'what does God's Word have to say about this' (insert whatever the topic is).

On that note, so often we hear about putting family first and prioritizing family time, but what does the bible actually say about family time?

Let's take a look at a few verses from the book of Ephesians:

- 5:22 – "Wives, submit yourselves to your own husbands as you do the Lord."
- 5:25 – "Husbands, love your wives, just as Christ loved the church and gave himself up for her."
- 6:1 – "Children, obey your parents in the Lord, for this is right."
- 6:4 – "Fathers, do not exasperate your children; instead, bring them up in the training and instruction of the Lord."

Now, this is not an all-inclusive list on what the bible says on this topic. However, I wanted to utilize these few key verses to make a point. Nothing listed in the verses above comes easily or just happens overnight. Doing these things, whether you are the husband, wife, parent, or child takes time, commitment, and effort.

You see, prioritizing family time isn't just about flowers, gifts, weekly date nights, or even family events. These things are great, but at the heart of it all, should be our obedience to God's Word. When each person in the home takes on their own God-given responsibility in their respective roles, everything tends to flow from there.

Whether you are married with kids, married with no kids, or single with kids, you have a role to play when it comes to nourishing relationships within your home. The problem is that very few Christians are abiding by these biblical principles. Submission is a hot topic especially for "modern-day Christian women". But, have we actually studied what that means or what it entails? Do we know why it's listed in the bible, why it's important, or how it benefits us? Do Christian men know what it really means to "love" their wives?

Submission and love go hand in hand when exhibited properly. But Christian couples are simply not taking the time to learn and develop these things. Which is why divorce rates are on a continual rise, and so many who remain married are miserable. The devil prides himself on destroying Christian marriages.

Similarly, that trickles down to the relationships with children in the home. Instead of parents teaching their kids *why* they should be obedient, most children today are left to themselves to learn a lot on their own. And as a result, disobedience is not only on the rise, but so many parents can't control their kids at all these days.

The bible is clear on our position as Christian parents. We should not only be teaching them about life, but we should be teaching them the Word of God! Now of course there are stories upon stories about "preacher's kids" who end up being the "worst of the worst". But, that is not an excuse for Christian parents not to do what God tells us to do in His Word regarding raising our children.

Doing our part doesn't guarantee our kids will turn out the best. However, doing our part does equal obedience to God.

Even if it's just the joy and peace of mind of knowing that you did what God told you to do, and having no guilt or shame about the end result, it's worth it to obey God.

The bible sets forth clear standards for relationships in the home. If we truly want to nourish those relationships the way God intended, then we absolutely MUST prioritize family time. In other words, make it a priority to work on your relationship with your spouse and/or your children. Put in the effort and time to submit, show love, teach your kids, and practice obedience to God.

Even if you are single and have no kids, take a look at the main verse for this chapter:

Philippians 2:4-5 (NLT) – "Don't look out only for your own interests, but take an interest in others, too. You must have the same attitude that Christ Jesus had."

Stop focusing on only what is important to you! If you haven't talked to your parents in a while, call them. Go visit. Go help out a grandparent, aunt, sister, or cousin, with a project they have been asking for assistance with. If you read all of Philippians chapter 2, you will see the specifics about the type of attitude that Jesus had that the verse above is referring to. You will see that Jesus had a humble and servant-like mentality. One in which his own comforts were set aside to help and serve others. Talk about things that are unheard of these days! Humility? Selflessness? Even Christians today, are all about me, myself, and I.

And this is where we let the devil, the world around us, and our flesh win. We let them dictate how we relate to people or not relate at all. As a result, there are failed marriages, ruined relationships with children, and family members that we haven't spoken to in years. This is not what God intended, nor does it typically lead to us enjoying our lives more.

Yes, there are circumstances and situations sometimes that we can't avoid, through no fault of own. However, those are the exceptions to the rule, and should not be the standard. If we begin to truly learn and put into practice what God says about nourishing our familial relationships, there is no way we won't begin to experience the fruits of that obedience.   All the blessings, the love, and all the enjoyment that comes with it!

As a single mother of a teenage boy, part of me used to dread having my son read a daily devotional, and then share with me what he learned. I dreaded it because it took time out of *my* evening. And after a long and hard day's work, I want nothing but to relax and do what pleases me. But, once I got over my selfishness, and disobedient attitude, I began to prioritize that time with my son.

Now 10 minutes a night has turned into 20-30 minutes of quality time where we have amazing conversations about God, His Word, and how it applies to my son's life. And to top it off, my son even enjoys it now too! Which if you have a teenager, you know that getting any time for a conversation is a feat in and of itself.

It's amazing what God can and will do in our lives, and in our relationships when we actually decide to take Him at His Word, obey and put it into practice!

Just remember not to push the biblical stuff aside to focus only on the physical and material things – gifts, money, going out, events, etc. When you build relationships God's way, all that other stuff will flow naturally as a result. You will *want* to spend more time with each other, and do things for one another.

What relationship(s) do you need to work on? How do you need to shift your priorities to include family time? Start today. I promise, it will be worth it and you will begin to enjoy your life more; even if it doesn't seem like it right now.

Putting it into Practice

- ➢ On a scale of 1-10, how would you currently rate "family time" in your home? With your spouse? Your kids? Extended family?
- ➢ Does your family time typically involve any of the biblical principles as set forth in God's Word that were mentioned in this chapter? Or just physical/material things?
- ➢ What areas specifically do you need to work on or start to make a priority?
- ➢ In what ways recently have you been selfish and only caring about what interests you?
- ➢ Take some time over the next 30 days to start shifting your schedule to prioritize more family time accordingly.

WARNING

Some family members will start off being annoyed when you start to utilize this product. They were perfectly fine NOT spending time with you, hearing from you, or being bothered by you at all! Do not let that deter you – as it is a trick of the enemy to get all of you comfortable and complacent about how distant the relationship has grown.

Consistent use of this product will deepen your relationships. You may even learn things you didn't want to learn (especially about your kids) – but stay the course. It will be worth it. Your home life will get significantly better and more enjoyable!

CHAPTER 14

Show Love to Everyone

For the whole law can be summed up in this one command:
Love your neighbor as yourself.

Galatians 5:14 (NLT)

With all the chaos, drama, violence, and craziness that goes on daily in the world around us, I often find solace in the fact that God's love never fails. No matter what is going on, God is always there. Here are some of my favorite verses regarding God's love for us as Christians:

- I John 4:9-10 – "This is how God showed his love among us: He sent his one and only Son into the world that we might live through him. This is love: not that we loved God, but that he loved us and sent his Son as an atoning sacrifice for our sins."
- Psalm 36:5 – "Your love, Lord, reaches to the heavens, your faithfulness to the skies."
- Romans 8:38-39 – "For I am convinced that neither death nor life, neither angels nor demons, neither the present nor the future, nor any powers, neither height nor depth, nor anything else in all creation, will be able to separate us from the love of God that is in Christ Jesus our Lord."

Not only does God love us, but He equips us by the power of his Holy Spirit to love others as well:

- Galatians 5:22-23 (NLT) – "But the Holy Spirit produces this kind of fruit in our lives: **love**, joy, peace, patience, kindness, goodness, faithfulness, gentleness, and self-control. There is no law against these things!"
- 2 Timothy 1:7 (NLT) – "For God has not given us a spirit of fear and timidity, but of power, **love**, and self-discipline."

In fact, as stated in the main verse for this chapter, God *commands* us to love others:

- John 13:34-35 – "A new command I give you: Love one another. As I have loved you, so you must love one another. By this everyone will know that you are my disciples if you love one another."
- I Corinthians 13:13 – "And now these three remain: faith, hope and love. But the greatest of these is love."

Showing love is the single most identifying factor that Christians can exhibit to share Christ with those around us. It's not our bumper stickers, our *What Would Jesus Do* bracelet, our 'Jesus Loves You' T-shirt, our church, or even the fact that we make it a point to read our bibles during our lunch breaks so people will see us. Those things help with our testimony, but as the saying goes, actions speak a lot louder than words (whether they are coming from our mouths or displayed on our clothes/cars).

What is it that makes showing love to one another so important, impactful, and unique? According to I Corinthians 13:1-8, here is what *true* love is:

"If I speak in the tongues of men or of angels, but do not have love, I am only a resounding gong or a clanging cymbal. If I have the gift of prophecy and can fathom all mysteries and all knowledge, and if I have a faith that can move mountains, but do not have love, I am nothing. If I give all I possess to the poor and give over my body to hardship that I may boast, but do not have love, I gain nothing.

Love is patient, love is kind. It does not envy, it does not boast, it is not proud. It does not dishonor others, it is not self-seeking, it is not easily angered, it keeps no record of wrongs. Love does not delight in evil but rejoices with the truth. It always protects, always trusts, always hopes, always perseveres. Love never fails."

Now does any of that sound like what you see on an everyday basis in the world around us? Absolutely not! In fact, it's quite the opposite. People are impatient, unkind, jealous, boastful, full of pride, selfish, angry, vengeful, gossipers, liars, and vain. And this is the norm.   This is why, when we exhibit true love, people will know there is something different about us. And this love isn't just for family and friends, or people we know. The bible says, 'love your neighbor as yourself'.

Our neighbor is any and everyone. That includes people you don't want to show love to – your boss, a mean co-worker, a homeless person on the street, your landlord, your bill collector, your ex-, even your enemies!

Matthew 5:43-47 (NLT) – "You have heard the law that says, 'Love your neighbor'[and hate your enemy. But I say, love your enemies! Pray for those who persecute you! In that way, you will be acting as true children of your Father in heaven. For he gives his sunlight to both the evil and the good, and he sends rain on the just and the unjust alike. If you love only those who love you, what reward is there for that? Even corrupt tax collectors do that much. If you are kind only to your friends, how are you different from anyone else? Even pagans do that."

Now *that* is something. Now do you see why people know you are under the influence of God when you display love like this?   It's because, it's not the norm. It's not easy, comfortable, or fun. But, God has given every Christian the power and capability to do it through His Holy Spirit that lives in us.

If we as Christians would step up to the plate, and love the way God commands us to, oh what an impact we would truly begin to make. In our homes, our neighborhoods, our schools, at work, in our communities, in our churches, in our cities, our states, our country, our world! So often we look for ways to make an impact, a difference, or a major change in the lives of those around us. The simplest and quickest place to start is by showing more love.

Go and be a blessing to someone who doesn't deserve it. Give someone $20 that already owes you and never paid you back. Donate a bag of clothes to the family whose kids get on your nerves the most in Sunday school. Pray for your ex-husband who just lost his job. Be polite and use your manners towards the co-worker who has been gossiping about you. Offer to give your uncle a ride to work, even though he has never helped you a day in his life.

And don't forget the simple everyday things like giving a stranger a smile in passing, sending an encouragement text to a friend, saying 'thank you' to the cashier in the store, calling a family member to say you were just thinking about them, giving the homeless person you pass every day that $10 bill that you've been holding on to.

There is a well-known movie called the *Pursuit of Happiness*, and there is no shortage of people running after that endeavor. The thing is, most often in life, we pursue the right things in the wrong ways, or for the wrong reasons. You see, when we shift our "pursuits" to the things that God tells us to do, all the other things we want or desire will begin to fall into place. In fact, if we truly love God, we will desire to do what pleases Him!

John 14:15 (NLT) – "If you love me, obey my commandments."

Matthew 6:33 (NLT) – "Seek the kingdom of God above all else, and live righteously, and he will give you everything you need."

You want to enjoy your life more? Then begin your journey on the road to the pursuit of showing love. Love God by learning His Word and practicing what it says. And love people – especially those who are seemingly
unlovable.

Just remember, God loves us despite our past, our sins, and the fact that we don't spend enough time with Him, or even enough time obeying Him. We are no more lovable than anyone else. And yet, God's love never fails us.

I John 4:19 says, "we love because He first loved us." In the same way that we don't deserve God's love, yet still reap the benefits of it daily, is the same way God wants us to go out and show more and more love every day, to everyone! Although it may be hard and even frustrating to start, I promise that showing love to everyone will begin to bring you a sense of joy and peace that you have never known.

Putting it into Practice

➤ When was the last time you showed love to someone you didn't know?

➤ Make a list of the people you are currently having a hard time showing love to.

➤ Use your list as a prayer list and start praying that God will begin to change your attitude and mind towards those people.

➤ Meditate on ALL the verses mentioned in this chapter and ask God to show you how to find ways to show love.

➤ Monitor your progress over the next 30 days and take note of the changes you are starting to see as you take steps towards showing more love.

WARNING

This love thing will begin to create some unwanted scrutiny. Family members and friends will begin to question you regarding your new pursuit. Most of all they will wonder 'why' – why your attitude has changed, why you are starting to be nice to certain people, why you are helping certain people, why you are showing love in general.

DO NOT be surprised if fellow Christians question you the most.

Non-Christians on the receiving end your love will no doubt be drawn to you. Be prepared to witness/testify about God and what He has done and is doing in your life. They will want to know, and you may lead some to a relationship with Christ!

NOTE: Extended use of this product can lead to overdose! You may start actively looking for people to love, to the point where you don't realize someone has cussed you out, thrown something at you, or slammed the door in your face.

CHAPTER 15

Extend Forgiveness

*Make allowance for each other's faults, and forgive anyone
who offends you. Remember, the Lord forgave you,
so you must forgive others.*

Colossians 3:13 (NLT)

It's time for yet another challenging topic – forgiveness. This plays a huge part in nourishing our relationships, because all of us at one point or another will need forgiveness. And just like showing love (as discussed in the previous chapter), we forgive others, because God forgave us. It really is that simple. But, as you and I know, it's those simple things that tend to be the most challenging for us as Christians.

Let's start with the basic definition of forgiveness. According to Websters dictionary the word forgive means to stop feeling angry or resentful toward someone for an offense, flaw, or mistake.   Easier said than done, right? Afterall, we all know there is a *wide* range of offenses, flaws, and mistakes!   So let's take a look at a few scriptures:

- Ephesians 1:6-8 – "to the praise of his glorious grace, which he has freely given us in the One he loves. In him we have redemption through his blood, the forgiveness of sins, in accordance with the riches of God's grace that he lavished on us. With all wisdom and understanding."
- I John 1:8-9 – "If we claim to be without sin, we deceive ourselves and the truth is not in us. If we confess our sins, he is faithful and just and will forgive us our sins and purify us from all unrighteousness."

Note that when it comes to God's forgiveness towards us, there are no stipulations regarding the level of offenses, flaws, or mistakes. Through His blood that was shed on the cross when Christ died for us, we have received forgiveness of ALL sins. And even as we continue to sin (which all of us will do by nature), when we confess our sins, God will continue to forgive us no matter what.

It is in light of God's forgiveness, that we are to extend forgiveness to others. And just like with love, this includes EVERYONE – no matter who the offender is, what the offense is, or how often the person offends you!

- Ephesians 4:32 – "Be kind and compassionate to one another, forgiving each other, just as in Christ God forgave you."
- Luke 6:37 – "Do not judge, and you will not be judged. Do not condemn, and you will not be condemned. Forgive, and you will be forgiven."
- Matthew 18:21-22 – "Then Peter came to Jesus and asked, 'Lord, how many times shall I forgive my brother or sister who sins against me? Up to seven times?' Jesus answered, 'I tell you, not seven times, but seventy-seven times'."
- Luke 17:3-4 – "So watch yourselves. If your brother or sister sins against you, rebuke them; and if they repent, forgive them. Even if they sin against you seven times in a day and seven times come back to you saying 'I repent,' you must forgive them."

The hardest part about forgiveness is letting go and moving past the hurt. We feel like forgiveness somehow lets people off the hook. That is not the case at all. Forgiveness isn't about absolving someone of their sins, nor does it necessarily pardon them from punishment. Remember, forgiveness is to stop harboring anger and resentment towards the people who have hurt us. When we extend forgiveness it's just as much for our benefit than the offender (if not more). Not to mention when we forgive, it is an act of obedience to God.

When we don't forgive, we dwell on our hurt and allow the negative feelings that come with it to fester and turn into bitterness, rage, hatred, etc. We actually end up hurting ourselves more than anything. Meanwhile, so often, the person who offended us has not only moved on with their life, but they are out enjoying their lives.

There are times where we won't get so much as an apology from the people who hurt us. There are other times where we feel wronged or hurt by someone and they honestly have no clue that they even offended us. Instead of pulling them aside and having a conversation with them about it, we allow bitterness to fester. And they are none the wiser. And then, there will be times where the person may go completely unpunished for what they did. In either case, we still can't let that hinder us from doing what God has commanded us to do.

Trust me, we all can name at least one person in our lives that seems impossible to forgive. In fact, if we are being honest, we don't really *want* to forgive them. As far as we are concerned, they don't deserve it. What we don't realize is that by not extending forgiveness, we hold on to all the negative feelings that come with that person. That whole situation. And until we deal with it, we will remain in bondage to it.

Some of us have been through some horrible and terrifying experiences that we never want to even think about again. Situations that have left some physical scars, emotional baggage, and mental and psychological trauma. Each of us has a story. I myself have been there and done that. Although, it does not happen overnight, what I can promise you is that, forgiveness is a big piece of the process, and a part of the road to healing.

We can only enjoy our lives but so much while carrying around a load of pain, hurt, anger, bitterness, and hatred. It may not be evident on the surface because some of us push it down so deep. But I promise you, it's there. You know, and the devil knows. Because he looks for opportunities to bring it up. To take you back to that very situation like it was yesterday. To dredge up the same emotions that come with it. And he will continue to do so successfully, until you take the first step and ask God to help you forgive whoever it is that you need to forgive.

And just like with everything else that God commands us to do, guess what? He will give you the power and strength through His Holy Spirit to be able to forgive also! God doesn't command us to do anything in His Word that He hasn't given us the capability to do. Let's not allow unforgiveness to hinder our prayers, blessings, or our walk with God.

Mark 11:24-25 (NLT) – "I tell you, you can pray for anything, and if you believe that you've received it, it will be yours. But when you are praying, first forgive anyone you are holding a grudge against, so that your Father in heaven will forgive your sins, too."

I like to remind myself of Jesus' attitude even while he literally hung on the cross as people were mocking him:

Luke 23:34 – "Jesus said, 'Father, forgive them, for they do not know what they are doing.' And they divided up his clothes by casting lots."

Extending forgiveness to those who were mocking him in the midst of his crucifixion! Now that is next level forgiveness right there! It's just a great reminder of how merciful, loving and forgiving God truly is!

Which brings me to my last point: There are also times where *we* are the offender. You know those *subtle hurts* that we may have forgotten about or tried to pretend never happened. The ex we constantly lied to. The friend we stabbed in the back. The co-worker we constantly gossip about. The neighbor we never speak to. The degrading tone in which we constantly talk to our children. The relative we have simply ignored or cut off for something they did 10 years ago. The person we borrowed money from and never paid back.

Yes, we too have hurt people. Intentionally and unintentionally. And we will need some forgiveness too.

Sometimes we will even need to forgive ourselves. People will hurt us, and we will hurt people. And all of us will sin and disobey God. Our job is to simply forgive. Confess your sins to God and ask for His forgiveness. Apologize when you hurt and offend others, and ask for their forgiveness. And pray to God for strength to take the necessary steps to forgive others who have hurt or offended you.

II Corinthians 2:6-8 – "The punishment inflicted on him by the majority is sufficient. Now instead, you ought to forgive and comfort him, so that he will not be overwhelmed by excessive sorrow. I urge you, therefore, to reaffirm your love for him."

Colossians 3:12-14 (NLT) – "Since God chose you to be the holy people he loves, you must clothe yourselves with tenderhearted mercy, kindness, humility, gentleness, and patience. Make allowance for each other's faults, and forgive anyone who offends you. Remember, the Lord forgave you, so you must forgive others. Above all, clothe yourselves with love, which binds us all together in perfect harmony."

Whether the person learns a lesson, feels guilt or shame, gets punished, or receives mercy, is in God's hands. But, forgiveness is a choice. One you will have to choose, in order to truly enjoy life the way God intended.

Putting it into Practice

- ➢ Take time to reflect on people you have hurt or offended. Who do you still need to apologize to and ask for forgiveness?
- ➢ Are there mistakes you have made that you need to forgive yourself for?
- ➢ What sins do you need to go to God about and ask for His forgiveness?
- ➢ Make a list of people you need to forgive and put a star next to those you find difficult to forgive.
- ➢ Meditate on the verses in this chapter and begin to commit your list to God in prayer. Ask God to give you the strength to be able to forgive.
- ➢ Give God time to work on your heart and move forward as He leads you.
- ➢ Take note of your progress along the way.

WARNING

This is a very serious product. However, when used properly it will reap some of the best benefits for your Christian journey.   It will be one of the absolute hardest products to utilize, but well worth it each time.

NOTE: once you start to use it consistently, people will begin to wonder about you.   Some may not even agree with your decision to exercise this product in some instances.   Both non-Christians and Christians alike sometimes don't understand why this is used on certain people.   Be prepared to stand your ground.

CHAPTER 16

Have Patience

Be completely humble and gentle; be patient,
bearing with one another in love.

Ephesians 4:2

On the coat tails of love and forgiveness, comes patience. We all know that none of these attributes develop overnight. Therefore, we must *learn* to have patience while we allow the Holy Spirit to do His work.

Patience is the capacity to accept or tolerate delay, trouble, or suffering without getting angry or upset. Now I know that nothing about that definition sounds fun or pleasant. In fact, none of us by nature like to wait – for anything. Our modern society caters to impatience by giving us so much at our fingertips. Through online shopping, we can literally place an order for food (groceries or take-out), toiletries, clothes or other items and have it delivered to us within 1-2 hours! And God forbid there be a delay. Our anger and emotions start to run rampant.

True patience, like love, really does come from the Holy Spirit:

Galatians 5:22-23 (NLT) – "But the Holy Spirit produces this kind of fruit in our lives: love, joy, peace, **patience**, kindness, goodness, faithfulness, gentleness, and self-control. There is no law against these things!"

Patience is something we work on and develop with God's help. And if we don't, then just like in the example above about waiting on a delivery, we will constantly be angry and frustrated whenever we don't get what we want when we want it. And impatient people do not live enjoyable lives.

As Christians, we have to learn to have patience with others, with ourselves, and even with God.

We have to allow time for the Holy Spirit to work in the lives of others, the same way we allow time for Him to work in our lives. So, don't expect your fellow brothers and sisters in Christ to get everything right all the time and right away. So often we are quick to point fingers and shift blame on others, while being quick to make excuses for ourselves when we do the exact or similar things. God's Word, calls for us to have patience with each other.

I Corinthians 13:4 – "Love is patient, love is kind. It does not envy, it does not boast, it is not proud."

Proverbs 14:29 – "Whoever is patient has great understanding, but one who is quick-tempered displays folly."

I Thessalonians 5:14 – "And we urge you, brothers and sisters, warn those who are idle and disruptive, encourage the disheartened, help the weak, be patient with everyone."

We must realize that as Christians we all have similar struggles. We struggle to love, to forgive, to not worry, to deal with anger, and other things. The last thing we need is to make it hard for each other. We are to encourage one another and have patience with one another. After all, we are in this Christian journey together.

Sometimes we even get into the habit of beating *ourselves* up when we fall short. But, we can't get stuck on our shortcomings, sins, flaws, or mistakes. Whether you make a mistake or someone else does – its ok. Show love, forgive, have patience, and move on. That really is the Christian life – a roller coaster journey of ups and downs. The more time we spend in God's Word and prayer, the more the Holy Spirit will begin to work in different areas of our lives. And the more "ups" we'll have on that roller coaster.

Now oftentimes, as Christians we will find ourselves in periods where we feel we are doing all we could possibly be doing regarding a situation. Yet we see no change. We start to wonder where God is and what He's up to. We start to lose patience. 'When Lord, when are you going to answer my prayer?' And this is where trusting and having faith in God is really put to a test.

> Psalm 37:7 – "Be still before the LORD and wait patiently for him; do not fret when people succeed in their ways, when they carry out their wicked schemes."

This verse deals with waiting on God to deal with those who hurt us. We should not get impatient or even anxious about people who seem to be "getting away with everything". God deals with people in His own way and in His own time. Our job is to leave it in His hands and go on doing the things God has told us to do – serve Him, live, and enjoy life.

If you know the story of Abraham, you know he was promised to be the father of many nations. He was 75 years old when God made the promise to him, and at the time he had no children. It wasn't until he was 100 years old that his wife Sarah finally gave birth to Isaac. If you do the math, that's 25 years that they waited on this promise that came directly from God! Most of us can barely wait 25 minutes for something we want, let alone 25 years. But, Abraham was a man of faith who trusted God:

> Hebrews 6:15 – "And so after waiting patiently, Abraham received what was promised."

You see, having patience is not only a command of God. It's not only something God empowers us through His Holy Spirit to do. It's something that when we exercise it, can develop our spiritual character and build our trust in God, as depicted by this beautiful passage of scripture:

> Romans 5:3-5 (TLB) – "We can rejoice, too, when we run into problems and trials, for we know that they are good for us—they help us learn to be patient. And patience develops strength of character in us and helps us trust God more each time we use it until finally our hope and faith are strong and steady. Then, when that happens, we are able to hold our heads high no matter what happens and know that all is well, for we know how dearly God loves us, and we feel this warm love everywhere within us because God has given us the Holy Spirit to fill our hearts with his love."

God doesn't make us wait for the sake of making us wait. God always has His master plan, and His own purpose for everything. As Christians, we must simply trust in Him while we wait.

Someone asked me once, 'what exactly do you do while you wait on God?' And my answer was: 'you do everything else you know to do; all the things He tells you to do from His Word.' Waiting patiently on God is not about just sitting around, staring out of a window, and waiting on a blessing to fall from the sky. Waiting is living every day in obedience to God, while trusting and having faith that He is working things out behind the scenes for your situation and circumstances.

What we often don't realize are the blessings that come along throughout the waiting process. The character He builds within us, the strength we develop by the power of His spirit, the increase in our level of faith, and those fruits of the spirit that start to show (love, joy, peace, self-discipline, etc.). One of my favorite verses expresses it best:

> Isaiah 40:3 – "But they that wait upon the LORD shall renew their strength; they shall mount up with wings as eagles; they shall run, and not be weary; and they shall walk, and not faint."

When we start to have patience with others, ourselves, and with God, we make room for God to make some amazing changes in our lives. We become like an eagle that soars through life, despite whatever is going on around them. You start to really enjoy life!

One of the hardest things for me personally to learn and accept was that I couldn't make things go my way all the time. That even when I seemingly had the best possible plan, which I had prayed about and everything, that God still could make adjustments. In fact, God could change the plan and timeline altogether!

Waiting and having patience is NOT easy. But, I do promise that it gets easier, the more you learn to do it. Just like everything else we have discussed in this book, patience can be developed. And once it is, you get to a point where you're simply ok with things being delayed or put on hold. Because you realize that God is in control and that His timing is perfect. You will even start to look for the things that God wants to show or teach you in the process of waiting.

Eventually, you stop being too hard on yourself for falling short. You stop giving up on people that fail or hurt you. You stop being angry at God for not answering a prayer right away. You learn to have patience. And when that happens, you begin to reap all the benefits and blessings that come along with it, including enjoying your life more!

Putting it into Practice

- ➢ Who are you currently struggling to have patience with? Why?
- ➢ Do you struggle with being patient with your own spiritual progress? In what areas are you being too hard on yourself?
- ➢ What things have you been waiting on God for? How has your attitude been in the process?
- ➢ Spend some time meditating on all the verses in this chapter. Ask God to help you and strengthen you to have more patience.
- ➢ As you begin to practice patience, take note of what God is teaching you through the waiting process, as well as, any changes you begin to see (physically, mentally, spiritually).

WARNING

Anytime you embark on the road to patience, you can ALWAYS count on any and everything imaginable to show up to test your patience. It will NOT be an easy journey. However, if you stay the course, the results and benefits will be more than worth it!

Continued use of this product will have people wondering why you are calmer than usual, and not losing your cool as much. You will sleep better at night as you begin to take some pressure off of yourself to be perfect, and just let God work in your life instead.   You will eventually begin to enjoy waiting on God and thus, enjoying all the things he is doing in your life along the journey to what you've asked Him for.

SECTION VI:

Live It Up!

This is the day which the Lord hath made;
we will rejoice and be glad in it.

Psalms 118:24

Every day that we wake up is a day to give God praise! No matter what your situation or circumstances are, it's important to give thanks and rejoice for each day that God blesses you with.

CHAPTER 17

Be Grateful

*Rejoice always, pray continually, give thanks in all circumstances;
for this is God's will for you in Christ Jesus.*

I Thessalonians 5:16-18

When you live in a world full of chaos and hatred, it can be hard to feel grateful sometimes. There are literally some days where life may genuinely seem to suck. Only recently has God really taught me to be grateful for His presence in my life. Grateful because I know that due to the relationship I have with Him, that I can go through some serious crap, but still be more than okay!

It's called an attitude of gratitude. It's a mindset really. One like everything else that has to be developed over time. And it starts with a shift in our focus.

Our natural tendency is to complain – about any, and everything. We can all find something to complain about if we look for it. However, when we shift our focus and begin to give thanks to God regardless of what is going on around us, do you know how much our lives will begin to change for the better?

Philippians 2:14 (TLB) – "In everything you do, stay away from complaining or arguing."

Psalm 118:29 – "Give thanks to the Lord, for he is good; his love endures forever."

I'm not saying all the bad stuff, heartache, frustrations, and pain will just vanish. But, our attitudes in the midst of life's toughest circumstances and situations will begin to shift dramatically.

Instead of stress, worry, doubt, anger, and bitterness, you'll start to see things that used to raise your tension levels, become less and less of a problem for you. People's harsh words and actions towards you, the car breaking down, getting sick, or your kids stressing you out, will no longer be *the end of the world.*

After all, if you look at the passage from I Thessalonians referenced at the head of this chapter, you'll see that being joyful always, praying continually, and giving thanks in all circumstances is actually God's will for us. And just think, we are always searching for God's will for our lives. Well this is one of several verses that tells us for sure what part of His will for us truly is.

God wants us to give thanks – to be grateful! I dare you to try it.

Psalm 147:7 – "Sing to the Lord with grateful praise."

Every day, even if it's only for a few minutes, take time to pause and give God praise. Talk to Him. Name several things you are grateful for. I'm grateful that He chose me before I was even born. That He destined me for a purpose. That He will never leave me. That He watches over me and protects me every day. That He comforts and guides me. That He actually listens and cares. That He loves me so much!

Usually around Thanksgiving time, I will have my Sunday school kids take a few minutes to write down as many things they can think of that they are thankful to God for. Afterwards, we all share our answers, and it's always so refreshing to hear everyone go through their lists.

Of course, there are always the common items across most lists such as: God, family, home, food, health, transportation, and clothes. Then there is the gratitude expressed for things that make certain individuals happy like: Starbucks coffee (me), Xbox games, cheer leading, music, favorite TV shows, and bubble baths. Then there are also the things that tend to get overlooked: the maintenance team for your apartment complex, best friends, education, the weather, intelligence, challenges that make us stronger, and opportunities to help others.

The list is endless when it comes to things to be grateful about. And being grateful and giving thanks is not just a seasonal thing to do every Thanksgiving Day. It is something we should be doing every day. After all, God's love is evident all day, every day, in everything, all around us. We never have to look far to see the goodness of God in our lives. Again, it's all about that shift in our focus.

So often we simply allow the not so good things going on to overshadow God's greatness in our lives.

We get so focused on what is wrong, what we don't have, what is broken, and how crazy things have become, that we forget that God is still in control.

Luke 1:37 (AMP) says, "For with God nothing [is or ever] shall be impossible." We must make a choice. Either complain, and be stressed all day about the fact that you had to deplete your savings to spend $1,000 on unexpected car repairs. OR, be grateful to God that you had the $1,000 in your savings to take care of the emergency in the first place.

People often say 'it can't get any worse'. Well I beg to differ, because things could absolutely be worse than what they are. I guarantee you, at any given moment, someone, somewhere is suffering or going through something far beyond what you are experiencing. Just watch the news at any point in the day. Trust me, there is a lot worse out there! It's all about perspective.

What I know, is that God is always at work in our lives as Christians. Sometimes even in ways we can't see. But, so often, He actually does work right before our very eyes for us to see clearly. Yet, we allow the enemy to twist our perspective and shift our mindset, to where we only see the negative side of the situation. Let's stop allowing our society, the devil, people, the internet, social media and any other outside influence to steal our praise or testimony.

God has been way too good to us, for us to be ungrateful.

One of my favorite old hymn songs is called *Count Your Blessings*. A portion of the lyrics say: "and it will surprise you what the Lord has done; count your blessings name them one by one; count your many blessings see what God has done!" I promise you, when you start to count and name your blessings, you will have very little time to complain and be stressed about all the crap going on in your life.

You want to enjoy your life more? Shift your focus and give God praise for what He has done, is doing, and has promised to do in your life!

Psalm 9:1 – "I will give thanks to you, Lord, with all my heart; I will tell of all your wonderful deeds."

And by the way, this attitude of gratitude should be extended not only to God, but to those He places in our lives to be a blessing to us as well. So, don't forget to show gratitude by saying 'thank you', giving a hug, a smile, a kiss, an encouraging text message or email, writing a letter, or giving a gift.

Let's make it our mission to stop complaining and learn to be grateful! It keeps our mind focused on thoughts of peace and joy instead of turmoil, our conversation positive, and creates an atmosphere that others around us can enjoy. Gratefulness is a key part of the lifestyle of one who truly enjoys life.

<u>*Putting it into Practice*</u>

➤ Take 5-10 minutes and just begin to list everything you can think of that you are grateful for.
➤ Now spend another 5-10 minutes reflecting on the list and literally giving thanks to God for everything you wrote down.
➤ Even if it's just for a few minutes each day, set some time aside for reflection to just write down what you are grateful for.
➤ What things are going on in your life right now that aren't so great? Pray about each situation and ask God to help you see the positive side, and also to find a resolution.

NOTE: sometimes the ONLY positive side is the fact that you know God is in control of it all and that nothing is impossible for Him.

➤ Other than God, who else do you need to express some gratitude to? Make a list of those you may have forgotten to thank recently, or someone who simply needs some encouragement. Go express some gratitude!

WARNING

This product is HIGHLY CONTAGIOUS!   An attitude of gratitude is like 'paying it forward'. The more you express it to others the more they will tend to express it as well!   Not to mention the more you use it, the more you will become addicted to using it on a daily basis.

Don't be surprised if you find yourself thanking your landlord, or the debt collector, or the guy who picks up your trash.

You may also notice that your problems will tend to fix themselves as you steer your focus away from them, and towards being grateful about the good things going on in your life instead.

CHAPTER 18

Laugh Like Crazy

*A cheerful heart is good medicine,
but a crushed spirit dries up the bones.*

Proverbs 17:22

Who doesn't enjoy a good ole hearty belly laugh? Even from a health standpoint, laughter in general is known to have amazing benefits both physically and mentally. It's one of the easiest and quickest methods of relief for stress and anxiety.

Have you ever been literally in tears, and then had a good friend say something that made you laugh? It's like an immediate high. And it helps you feel better right away, even if only for a few seconds or minutes. The bible says, "a cheerful heart is good medicine". In other words, laughter does the body and mind good!

Think about what makes you laugh – irony, sarcasm, comedy, jokes, people, TV shows, facial expressions, music, etc. Think about those moments when you laugh the most. Think about what you're doing when you laugh, who you're with, and what triggers your laughter. Now, start making it a point to ensure you put yourself in that particular environment more often.

You see, God has not called us to a life of misery where we frown, pout, and walk around looking frustrated and angry all the time. He has called us to be full of love, peace, and joy. And joyful people smile. They laugh! Just like with being grateful, we have to learn to laugh more!

As you learned in the last chapter, I promise you that once you start counting your blessings, you'll be reminded of where God has brought you from. You'll remember the stuff you used to do, the things you used to say, the way you used to act, and the decisions you used to make.

I often go back and read old journals from my late teenage and college years. And let me tell you, it absolutely cracks me up! You will laugh at your progress, to the point where you cry happy tears. Just like we have things to be grateful for, we have so many reasons to just smile. To burst into laughter.

Psalm 126:2-3 – "Our mouths were filled with laughter, our tongues with songs of joy. Then it was said among the nations, 'The LORD has done great things for them.' The LORD has done great things for us, and we are filled with joy."

If you pay attention, you will often see that it's almost as if God has a sense of humor. He has a habit of doing great and mighty things that make people laugh in disbelief, because it seems so impossible. Remember God's promise to Abraham to make him a father of many nations, when he was already 100 years old and had no kids at the time.

Genesis 17:17 – "Abraham fell facedown; he laughed and said to himself, 'Will a son be born to a man a hundred years old? Will Sarah bear a child at the age of ninety?'"

How about Job who literally lost everything. But, in the midst of it, was counseled by one of friends as follows:

Job 8:21 – "He will yet fill your mouth with laughter and your lips with shouts of joy."

Several times before Jesus performed a miracle, he was laughed at and ridiculed.

Matthew 9:24 – "he said, 'Go away. The girl is not dead but asleep." But they laughed at him.

In each instance we know God being God, came through and did what was seemingly impossible. He not only blessed Abraham with a son, but gave him several children, through whose lineage came our Savior, Jesus Christ. God ended up blessing the second part of Job's life more than the first. And the girl that was presumed dead, Jesus raised back to life.

We have instances in our lives where God turned our situation completely around for good. Where everything that could go wrong, went wrong all at the same time. A serious illness. A financial burden. A legal matter. Our lives at risk. It's those instances that He brings us through, and we look back at in retrospect, and are so in awe of His grace, that we literally break out in laughter and joy! Because God is that good and amazing! And because we so often go through so much just to get to that point of blessing, it makes it all the more reason to break out in praise!

Luke 6:21 – "Blessed are you who hunger now, for you will be satisfied. Blessed are you who weep now, for you will laugh."

Ecclesiastes 3:3-5 – "a time to weep and a time to laugh, a time to mourn and a time to dance"

Some of us have gone through so much that we could literally write a book about it! There have been times in our lives where it really was a time to cry and mourn. And those times were tough.

Which is why when God brings us through it, we have to celebrate. We have to dance. We have to laugh.

We may not always *feel* like smiling or laughing. In fact, Proverbs 14:13 says, "Even in laughter the heart may ache, and rejoicing may end in grief." However, laughter is a part of our Christian journey.

Sometimes, you will have to proactively find ways to produce that 'cheerful heart' that our header verse talks about. If it is the people you are with that are bringing your mood down, then find someone else to hang out with. If what you are watching on TV, reading on the internet or social media, or listening to on the radio has you upset and in a bad mood, then change it! Turn the channel to one of your favorite sitcoms. Close out of the internet and get off social media for a bit. Go read a book instead (like this one). Create an upbeat music playlist.

Most people that know me, will tell you I have no problem spending time by myself. I'm famous for entertaining myself and finding things to keep me laughing – a movie, music, memes, etc. You can even download an app on your phone for daily jokes!

Do yourself a favor and make it a point to find things that uplift your spirit, cheer you up, and make you laugh daily. I guarantee that adding more laughter into your day will help you to enjoy your life more.

Putting it into Practice

- On a scale of 1-10, with 10 being the highest, how would you rate how often you spend laughing?
- What are the top 5 things or people that make you laugh?
- Can you think of 2-3 things lately that God has done in your life that puts a smile on your face or laughter in your heart? It may help to reflect on some of the things we have covered in this book and the practice assignments that came with it.
- Start setting aside at least a 10-15 minute period each day where you sit and do something that lifts your spirits and makes you laugh. Schedule it in your phone or on your calendar as a reminder if necessary.
- Meditate on the verses used in this chapter. In your prayer time, ask God to help you laugh more and have a cheerful heart.

WARNING

Use of this product will have you laughing at odd times. People will think you are slightly crazy. But, don't let that hinder you or make you scared to just let the laughter flow.

NOTE: this product can also become very addictive; even to the point where you find yourself laughing when most think you should be crying or punching a wall. But, it's ok to abuse this product in that sense. In fact, over laughing is encouraged, as it will work wonders for your physical and mental well-being.

DO NOT stop using this product once it begins to give the desired effects. You can never outgrow it, and it is not something your body will become immune to over time.

CHAPTER 19

Celebrate All Success

*He holds success in store for the upright, he is a shield
to those whose walk is blameless.*

Proverbs 2:7

Throughout this entire book, we've been discussing ways to enjoy life more as a Christian. Each of those ways, has involved dependence upon the Holy Spirit within us, as well as, our resolve to spend more time reading and learning God's Word. As stated previously, spiritual growth is a lifelong process. It doesn't matter how long you have been a Christian. God is constantly working on us to be more Christ-like, and will continue to do so until we join Him in heaven.

> Philippians 1:6 – "being confident of this, that he who began a good work in you will carry it on to completion until the day of Christ Jesus."

In case you haven't figured it out yet, spiritual growth is the *true* success that God wants us to attain.

> Ecclesiastes 12:13 – "Now all has been heard; here is the conclusion of the matter: Fear God and keep his commandments, for this is the duty of all mankind."

The main goal of Christianity is to fear God (reverence, respect, and serve Him) and obey His Word. How well we do that is the true measure of success for Christians!

The house, car, college degrees, money, accolades, and anything else you can name are simply by-products. Because spiritual growth is a lifelong process, it is all the more important to celebrate our success along the way. We have to track our progress as we go. Recognize where we started, what we've accomplished so far, and how much further we have to go, so we can continue to push towards our goal daily.

Maybe you never used to have devotions, but now you're doing it three times a week. Or maybe you never used to pray apart from saying grace at the dinner table, and now you have a set time each morning. Maybe you've decided to let this year be the first year that you read through the bible. Or maybe you've decided to work on your anger issues, so you looked up every verse you could find about anger to see what God has to say about it. Maybe you never used to put money in the offering plate, and now you're making it a point to give something every time you go to church.

Whatever the case, track your success. All the little assignments from the 'Putting it into Practice' sections at the end of each chapter are there for a reason. Trust me, you will want to reflect back on them as a point of reference. Just like with any other goal, tracking your success is a huge motivational factor to keep you moving in the right direction. It shows you what God has done, and gets you excited to see what He is going to do next in your life!

Our success can also be a motivational factor to those around us. Your spiritual growth could motivate someone else to work on their relationship with God. Or better yet, a non-Christian co-worker, neighbor, relative or friend may give their lives to Christ because of the changes they see in you!

Now, I don't want to overshadow success in other areas of our lives. It's just that our society tends to associate success with material things. Whether it's being famous, having a ton of money, owning several businesses, multiple homes or cars, having thousands of followers on social media, getting a national award, or getting a doctor's degree.

Material things are certainly considered blessings, and can be "a" measure of success. However, they are not, nor should they ever be "the" measure of true success for Christians.

Just remember that by putting God first, you absolutely can't go wrong! When we do things God's way, He takes care of us. and gives us success in all the other ways that matter. Here is some spiritual food for thought:

Joshua 1:7-8 – "Be strong and very courageous. Be careful to obey all the law my servant Moses gave you; do not turn from it to the right or to the left, **that you may be successful wherever you go**. Keep this Book of the Law always on your lips; meditate on it day and night, so that you may be careful to do everything written in it. **Then you will be prosperous and successful.**"

II Chronicles 26:5 – "He sought God during the days of Zechariah, who instructed him in the fear of God. **As long as he sought the Lord, God gave him success.**"

Proverbs 2:7 – "**He holds success in store for the upright**, he is a shield to those whose walk is blameless."

Ways to Celebrate

The actual act of celebrating is the fun part. It's when we literally take some time to acknowledge and rejoice about our progress. No matter how you choose to celebrate, always start by giving thanks to God. Remember, that it's only by His power and grace that we do what we do. And, it is very important to give praise and thanks to God EVERY step of the way.

Things that can be done to celebrate your success in your Christian journey are:

- share the news with others (accountability partners, family, friends)
- make it an event - throw a "progress party"
- treat yourself to a "cheat day" - go off your diet, have a drink, or skip the gym
- take a mental health day off from work
- go and do something you enjoy

Regardless of how you celebrate, just remember to be sure to celebrate even the small achievements. Every little thing we accomplish along the way for God is worth celebrating and getting excited about!

Remember that God wants us to be successful Christians.

Regardless of your ethnicity, gender, background, profession, educational level, social status, bank account balance, or where you live - if you belong to God, He wants you to be successful in Him. Thankfully, God's measure of success is not dependent on any of the ways that the world measures success! In fact, He gives us everything we need to be successful.

The world says go to college and get a good education, get a high paying job so you can make a ton of money, buy anything you want, do what you want, when you want, how you want, and you will be successful. There is no need for God. But the bible says, seek God first and foremost, learn and obey His Word, commit your goals to Him, include Him in everything you do, and He will bless you and give you success spiritually and in all other aspects of your life as well.

> **Matthew 16:26 (AMP)** – "For what will it profit a man if he gains the whole world (wealth, fame, success), but forfeits his soul? Or what will a man give in exchange for his soul?"

Don't miss out on the true blessings of this life. Don't get so caught up in all the craziness going on in the world that you neglect your relationship with God, and keep yourself from true success. We all know that life is short, and tomorrow is not promised to anyone. So whether it's a work day, vacation day, the weekend, or you're sick and shut in - make every day count as a success by spending time with God, living for Him, and truly enjoying life! And, make it your duty to celebrate along the way!

Putting it into Practice

- ➤ Take some time and reflect on your Christian journey thus far (regardless of how long it has been). Make a list of all the success (that you can think of) that you have had thus far in all areas of your life – spiritually, physically, financially, your family, your home, your career, your education, etc.
- ➤ After completing your list, spend time in prayer giving God praise for everything He has done in your life.
- ➤ Then, plan a way to celebrate your past success. It can be anything big or small that works for you.
- ➤ As you remember things God has done in your life or other successes you have had, add them to your list accordingly. And going forward, continue to add to your list as you continue to experience new success.
- ➤ Make it a point (whether weekly or monthly) to genuinely take some time and celebrate all the good things God is doing in your life. Remember the celebration can be something simple (i.e. treat yourself to something you enjoy) or something big depending on the occasion (i.e. a party to celebrate you getting your Master's degree).

WARNING

Some people will NOT want to celebrate with you. In fact, some will be confused, jealous, and even upset by your success – Christians and non-Christians alike. Do not let this deter you from giving praise to God and celebrating. This product can be utilized in an individual and/or group setting. However, it is often used alone – and that's ok!

Don't be afraid to use this on even the smallest of successes. Going a whole day without snapping on your kids, cursing, or eating sweets, does count!

Side effects of this product include, but are not limited to: happy crying, laughter, intense feelings of joy, the sensation to want to dance or do cartwheels, outbursts of happiness, and increased levels of excitement in general.

CHAPTER 20

Do What You Enjoy

Command those who are rich in this present world not to be arrogant nor to put their hope in wealth, which is so uncertain, but to put their hope in God, who richly provides us with everything for our enjoyment.

I Timothy 6:17

Throughout this book, we have covered so many ways in which we can begin to enjoy our lives as Christians more: cultivating our faith by spending more time with God, acknowledging life's challenges, checking our emotions, remembering self-care, and nourishing our relationships.

I know some of you are thinking, this is not exactly what I was looking for in regards to 'enjoying life'. Where is the fun stuff? Where is the stuff that I can really get excited about? Can I bypass all this spiritual stuff like reading the bible, prayer, dealing with worry, anger, past mistakes, working on self-discipline, showing love, forgiveness, patience, and gratitude?

The answer is yes.

If you want, you can ignore half, if not all, of the things mentioned in this book. In fact, you can continue to live life exactly the way you do right now. But, the thing is, when we as Christians try to live life without incorporating God into it, we miss out on so many things – blessings, answered prayers, success, peace, and true enjoyment (just to name a few).

If you think you are living it up now, I promise you (and I say this definitively) that when you start to incorporate the things listed in this book, that you will begin to experience life in a whole new way. The level of enjoyment that living life *with* God brings cannot be fully put into words. Absolutely NOTHING can compare to the love, joy, and peace that you get by living life God's way.

The problem is, the world, our flesh, and our enemy the devil are all set up to steer us as far away from the things of God as they possibly can. Christians are actually deceived into thinking they don't need God as much as the bible says we do. We equate Christianity and the bible with rules and regulations. Rules and regulations that will somehow *ruin* the way we want to live our lives, mess up our fun, or kill our enjoyment. But, Jesus specifically stated in John 10:10 (AMP):

> "The thief comes only in order to steal and kill and destroy. **I came that they may have and enjoy life**, and have it in abundance [to the full, till it overflows]."

God's intention was that we would not only exist on earth as non-believers do, but that we would truly live and enjoy life. And we only do that to the fullest by living life in Him, and according to His Word.

Yes, there are rules. But the main rule, is simply, to grow in our faith and become more like Christ. By doing this, we don't lose out or set aside our enjoyment of other things. Just as our header verse states from I Timothy 6:17, God richly provides us with everything for our enjoyment!

As Christians we have to stop being deceived into thinking that life with God is no fun.

I'll even go as far to say, that we don't even *know* the meaning of real fun and enjoyment *until* we give God a chance to work in our lives! Let's take a look at several verses to see exactly what the bible has to say about enjoyment:

- Deuteronomy 6:1-2 – "These are the commands, decrees and laws the LORD your God directed me to teach you to observe in the land that you are crossing the Jordan to possess, so that you, your children and their children after them may fear the LORD your God as long as you live by keeping all his decrees and commands that I give you, **and so that you may enjoy long life."**

- I Chronicles 29:26-28 – "David son of Jesse was king over all Israel. He ruled over Israel forty years—seven in Hebron and thirty-three in Jerusalem. **He died at a good old age, having enjoyed long life, wealth, and honor.** His son Solomon succeeded him as king."

- Nehemiah 8:10 – "Nehemiah said, "**Go and enjoy choice food and sweet drinks,** and send some to those who have nothing prepared. This day is holy to our Lord. Do not grieve, for the joy of the LORD is your strength."

- Psalm 37:3 – "Trust in the LORD and do good; dwell in the land and **enjoy safe pasture.**"

- Psalm 37:18-19 – "The blameless spend their days under the LORD's care, and their inheritance will endure forever. In times of disaster they will not wither; **in days of famine they will enjoy plenty.**"

- Ecclesiastes 8:15 – "**So I commend the enjoyment of life,** because there is nothing better for a person under the sun than to eat and drink and be glad. **Then joy will accompany them in their toil all the days of the life** God has given them under the sun."

- Isaiah 3:10 – "Tell the righteous it will be well with them, **for they will enjoy the fruit of their deeds.**"

- Jeremiah 31:5 – "Nevertheless, I will bring health and healing to it; **I will heal my people and will let them enjoy abundant peace and security.**"

- Acts 2:46-47 – " Every day they continued to meet together in the temple courts. They broke bread in their homes and ate together with glad and sincere hearts, **praising God and enjoying the favor of all the people.** And the Lord added to their number daily those who were being saved."

- Acts 9:31 – "**Then the church throughout Judea, Galilee and Samaria enjoyed a time of peace and was strengthened**. Living in the fear of the Lord and encouraged by the Holy Spirit, it increased in numbers."

- Romans 15:24 – "I plan to do so when I go to Spain. I hope to see you while passing through and to have you assist me on my journey there, **after I have enjoyed your company for a while**."

Don't tell me that God doesn't want us to enjoy the things of life. God wants us to enjoy people, the fruit of our labor, peace, favor, food and drink, safety, and even wealth and honor. He NEVER states that these things are out of our reach, or that we shouldn't have them. But, if you take notice and actually read these verses in context, you will see that in each instance, the individuals involved in each verse mentioned, enjoyed these things as a result of obeying and serving God!

If you ask me, we are the ones who hinder our enjoyment of life.

You want to truly enjoy your life more? Start incorporating the things in this book (all of which are based on scripture), and I guarantee you will begin to see immediate results! In fact, not only will you start to experience more joy in your life, but God will start to give you more *time* to do the things you enjoy. All that time you used to spend being angry, stressed, worried, and dwelling on the past, can now be better spent on you growing your relationship with God and enjoying life.

You see, as I grow in my walk with God, He's actually helping me and teaching me to do more of the things that bring me joy. So now, onto the fun part that you've been waiting for. What is it you actually enjoy doing? Or better yet, what do you wish you had time to do but never seem to be able to? Have you ever made a list?

Here are some of the things I enjoy:

- a bubble bath
- red wine just before bed
- trying out a new restaurant
- roller coasters

- binge watching shows on Netflix
- Sunday afternoon naps after church
- intense workouts because they help me relieve stress
- a hot-stone massage
- taking 15 minute meditation walks
- relaxing and listening to music
- Italian food – pasta will forever be my weakness!
- writing in my journal
- playing cards and board games
- playing pool
- zip-lining
- going to the theater to see a good action movie
- trying to cook new recipes
- traveling to places I've never been
- gospel concerts
- Starbucks – Caramel Macchiato's all the way – hot or iced!

Thank you God, for these enjoyable pleasures!

Whether it's prayer time during those first few quiet moments of your day when you first wake up, your favorite latte, or listening to your song of the week on the radio, giving your child a huge hug, texting a romantic message to your significant other, watching the sunset, visiting friends, or painting – find and enjoy those moments of peace and happiness throughout your day or week. Life is too short, for us to overlook, miss out on, and not enjoy the precious moments that God gives us each day for our enjoyment.

Make it your mission today to learn to love God's Word, grow in your walk with Him, and enjoy life to the fullest!

Putting it into Practice

➤ Take some time and look up the verses listed in this chapter. Read them in context (i.e. the surrounding verses or the full chapter) to get an even better understanding of the point being made.

➤ Make a decision today, on whether or not you want to transition to truly enjoying your life more or not. If the answer is yes, then pray about it and begin to implement the things listed in this book. NOTE: you may have to read it again or several times – and that's ok!

➤ Make a list of the things you enjoy doing. Include the things you wish you had more time to do or want to try.

➤ Start incorporating the things on your list into your calendar – whether daily, weekly, monthly or as a planned event or vacation.

➤ Start tracking how much more time you are spending enjoying life, as you continue to spend more time in God's Word and grow in your relationship with Him.

WARNING

Use of this product can be become addictive. However, when used often or in large doses, it will not cause you harm.

NOTE: Continued use may also draw attention from others, causing them to want to participate. Some will question how you find the time to use the product so much, and may even become jealous.

Side effects include, but are not limited to: increased feelings of relaxation, calmness, physical bursts of energy, an overall good mood, a positive mindset, and an attitude of 'not caring' about your problems.

ENDNOTES

Tracy M. Sumner, *Bible Vitals* (Barbour Publishing, 2010)

Pamela L. McQuade, *The Complete People & Places of the Bible* (Barbour Publishing, 2014)

"devour." *Merriam-Webster.com.* 2020. https://merriam-webster.com (6 January 2020).

Joyce Meyer, *Battlefield of the Mind* (Faith Words Edition, 1995)

"forgive." *Merriam-Webster.com.* 2020. https://merriam-webster.com (20 July 2020).

"patience." *Merriam-Webster.com.* 2020. https://merriam-webster.com (1 August 2020).

Johnson Oatman, "Count Your Blessings", *Hymnary.org.* 2020. https://hymnary.org (13 November 2020)

ACKNOWLEDGEMENTS

I give all praise and glory first and foremost to God. Without Him I am nothing. I continue to be amazed at his unfailing love for me every day. Thank you Lord, for your Son, Jesus Christ who died on the cross for my sins. Thank you for the opportunity to be used as a vessel of glory and honor for your namesake. I pray this book will be the first of many that will encourage, motivate, and inspire others to learn to love your Word and enjoy life the way you intended.

To my son Korboi; whose very existence is my motivator to push to be the Christian mother and woman that God has called me to be. It's been you, me and God for some time now. And now my favorite sidekick is a teenager! I'm so grateful for who you are, and excited about the young man God is molding you to be, and what He has in store for your life. Our devotional and prayer time, as well as, our conversations about life in general, have been some of the most cherished moments and best part about being your mom. I hope you always remember to put God first and continue to seek Him through His Word. I love you kid!

A special thank you to Aerie; my cousin, my friend, my confidante, and my support person. Words cannot express how much of a blessing you have been in this stage of my life. It was your ongoing support to pursue my dreams and goals, that kept me encouraged and motivated to launch my blog, my online course, and now this book! Thank you for listening, making me laugh, praying for me, encouraging me, not judging me, giving me a key to your place when I needed to just 'get away', and for being the angel that I needed in the lowest point of my life. You are awesome and I thank God for you every day! I love you cous!

To my sister Faith, my niece Quianday, my extended family members, my friends, and my church family at New Life Baptist Church, I say thank you all. Your presence, support, and most of all, your prayers, have been everything to me over these last eight years since I have relocated back to VA. I love and cherish you all!

ABOUT THE AUTHOR

Demetra Muingbeh is a Christian single mother who resides in Richmond, VA with her son. She loves God and His Word, and is a fanatic about teaching and motivating others to learn God's Word and enjoy life to the fullest!

She graduated with a B.S. in Biblical Studies from Philadelphia Biblical University (now Cairn University). She has since worked with churches and non-profit organizations in various capacities. Her passion is teaching, training, and coaching in general.

She publishes inspirational posts and resources on her blog *In the Mirror of God*, where you can also get access to her free online course *Learning the Bible 101: Benefits, Methods & Hindrances,* upon subscribing.

BEFORE YOU GO . . .

- Share or tweet that you finished *20 Ways to Enjoy Your Life More As A Christian*

- Write a review on Amazon.com

- Connect with Demetra via email - deme@inthemirrorofgod.com

- Visit her blog and learn about her online ministry at www.inthemirrorofGod.com
    - Like and follow *In the Mirror of God* on Facebook and Pinterest
    - Instagram - @inthemirrorofGod
    - Twitter - @DemeITMOG